The Roundheads;
or, The Good Old Cause

Aphra Behn

THE ROUNDHEADS
OR, The Good Old Cause

Aphra Behn

1682

CONTENTS

ACT I.

    Scene I

ACT II.

    Scene I

ACT III.

    Scene I

    Scene II

ACT IV.

    Scene I

    Scene II

    Scene III

    Scene IV

ACT V.

    Scene I

    Scene II

    Scene III

    Scene IV

    Scene V

The Roundheads; or, The Good Old Cause

ACT I.

Scene I.

The Street.

Enter three Souldiers, and Corporal Right.

Cor.
Ah Rogues, the World runs finely round, the bus'ness is done.

1 Sould.
Done, the Town's our own, my fine Rascal.

2 Sould.
We'll have Harlots by the Belly, Sirrah.

1 Sould.
Those are Commodities I confess I wou'd fain be trucking for,—but no words of that Boy.

Cor.
Stand, who go's there?

To them a Joyner and Felt-maker.

1 Sould.
Who are you for,—hah?

Joyn.
Are for Friend; we are for Gad and the Lord *Fleetwood*.

1 Sould.
Fleetwood, knock 'em down, *Fleetwood* that snivelling Thief?

Felt.
Why Friends, who are ye for?

The Roundheads; or, The Good Old Cause

Cor.
For? who shou'd we be for, but *Lambert*, Noble *Lambert*? Is this a time o'th' day to declare for *Fleetwood*, with a Pox? indeed. i'th morning 'twas a Question had like to have been decided with push a Pike.

2 Sould.
Dry blows wou'd ne'r a don't, some must have sweat blood for't, but—'tis now decided.

Joyn.
Decided!

2 Sould.
Yes, decided Sir, without your Rule for't.

Joyn.
Decided? by whom Sir? by us the Free-born Subjects of *England* , by the Honourable Committee of Safety, or the Right Reverend City? without which Sir, I humbly conceive, your Declaration for *Lambert* is illegal, and against the Property of the People.

2 Sould.
Plain *Lambert*; here's a sawcy Dog of a Joyner; Sirrah, get ye home, and mind your Trade, and save the Hang-man a labour.

Joyn.
Look ye, Friend, I fear no Hang-man in Christendom; for Conscience and Publick good, for Liberty and Property, I dare as far as any man.

2 Sould.
Liberty and Property, with a pox, in the mouth of a Joyner; you are a pretty Fellow to settle the Nation,—what says my Neighbour Felt-maker?

Felt.
Why verily, I have a high respect for my honourable Lord *Fleetwood* , he is my intimate Friend, and till I find his Party the weaker, I hope my Zeal will be strengthened for him.

The Roundheads; or, The Good Old Cause

2 Sould.
Zeal for *Fleetwood*, Zeal for a Halter, and that's your due: Why, what has he ever done for you? Can he lead you out to Battel? Can he silence the very Cannon with his Eloquence alone?—Can he talk—or fight—or—

Felt.
But verily he can pay those that can, and that's as good—and he can pray—

2 Sould.
Let him pray, and we'll fight, and see whose bus'ness is done first; We are for the General, who carries charms in every syllable; can act both the Souldier and the Courtier, at once expose his Breast to dangers for our sakes—and tell the rest of the pretending Slaves a fair Tale, but hang 'em sooner than trust 'em.

1 Soul.
Ay, ay, a *Lambert*, a *Lambert*, he has courage, *Fleetwood*'s an Ass to him.

Felt.
Hum—here's Reason Neighbour.

        [to the Joyner.

Joyn.
That's all one, we do not act by reason.

Corp.
Fleetwood's a Coward.

2 Sould.
A Blockhead.

1 Sould.
A snivelling Fool; a General in the Hangings, no better.

The Roundheads; or, The Good Old Cause

Joyn.
What think ye then of *Vane*?

2 Sould.
As of a Fool, that has dreamt of a new Religion, and only fit to reign in that Fifth Monarchy he preaches so much up; but no King in this Age.

Felt.
What of *Hasterig*?

2 Sould.
A Hangman for *Hasterig*, I cry, No, no, One and all, a *Lambert*, a *Lambert*; he is our General, our Protector, our King, our Keiser, our — even what he pleases himself.

1 Sould.
Well, if he pleases himself he pleases me.

2 Sould.
He's our Rising Sun, and we'll adore him, for the Speaker's Glory's set,

Cor.
At nought, Boyes; how the Rogue look'd when his Coach was stop'd.

Joyn.
Under favour, what said the Speaker?

2 Sould.
What said he? prethee what cou'd he say that we wou'd admit for Reason? Reason and our bus'ness are two things: Our Will was Reason and Law too,' and the Word of Command lodg'd in our Hilts: *Cobbet* and *Duckenfield* show'd 'em Cock-pit Law.

Cor.
He understood not Souldiers Dialect; the Language of the Sword puzled his Understanding; the Keeneness of which, was too sharp

for his Wit, and over-rul'd his Roles—therefore he very mannerly kiss'd his hand, and wheel'd about,—

2 Sould.
To the place from whence he came,

Cor.
And e're long, to the Place of Execution.

1. Sould.
No, damn him, he'll have his Clergy.

Joy.
Why is he such an Infidel to love the Clergy?

Cor.
For his Ends: But come, lets go drink the General's Health; *Lambert!* not *Fleetwood*, that Son of a Custard, always quaking.

2 Sould.
Ay, ay, *Lambert* I say,—besides, he's a Gentleman.

Felt.
Come, Come, Brother Souldier, let me tell you, I fear you have a *Stewart* in your Belly.

Cor.
I am sure you have a Rogue in your Heart, Sirrah, which a Man may perceive through that sanctify'd Dogs Face of yours; and so get ye gone ye Rascals, and delude the Rabble with your canting Politicks.

[*Every one beats 'em.*

Felt.
Nay, and you be in Wrath, I'll leave you.

Joy.
No matter Sir, I'll make you know I'm a Free-born Subject, there's Law for the Righteous Sir, there's Law.

The Roundheads; or, The Good Old Cause

[*Go out.*

Cor.
There's Halters ye Rogues?—

2 Sould.
Come Lads, let's to the Tavern, and drink Success to change; I doubt not but to see 'em chop about, till it come to our great Heroe again.— Come, to the Tavern.

Going out, are met by Loveless and Freeman who enter, and stay the Corporal.

Cor.
I'll follow ye Comrade presently.

[*Ex. the rest of the Souldiers,*

Save ye noble Collonel.

Free.
How is't Corporal?

Cor.
A brave World Sir, full of Religion, Knavery, and Change; we shall shortly see better days.

Free.
I doubt it Corporal;

Cor.
I'le warrant you Sir,—but have you had never a Billet, no Present, nor Love-remembrance to day, from my good Lady *Desbro*?

Free.
None, and wonder at it: Hast thou not seen her Page to day?

Cor.
Faith Sir I was imploy'd in Affairs of State, by our Protector that shall be, and could not call.

Free.
Protector that shall be? who's that, *Lambert* or *Fleetwood* , or both?

Cor.
I care not which, so it be a Change; but I mean the General?—but Sir, my Lady *Desbro* is now at Morning Lecture here hard by, with the Lady *Lambert*.

Lov.
Seeking the Lord for some great Mischief or other.

Free.
We have been there, but could get no Opportunity of speaking to her,—*Loveless*, know this Fellow,—he's honest and true to the Heroe, though a *Red-Coat*? I trust him with my Love, and have done with my Life.

Lov.
Love! Thou can'st never make me believe thou art earnestly in Love with any one of that damn'd Reformation.

Free.
Thou art a Fool; where I find Youth and Beauty, I adore, let the Saint be true or false.

Lov.
'Tis a Scandal to one of us to converse with 'em; they are all sanctify'd *Jilts*; and there can be neither Credit nor Pleasure in keeping 'em Company; and 'twere enough to get the Scandal of an Adherer to their devilish Politicks to be seen with 'em.

Free.
What, their Wives?

Lov.
Yes, their Wives. What see'st thou in 'em but Hypocrisie? Make Love to 'em, they answer you in Scripture.

The Roundheads; or, The Good Old Cause

Free.
Ay, and lye with you in Scripture too. Of all Whores, give me your zealous Whore; I never heard a Woman talk much of Heaven, but she was much for the Creature too. What do'st think I had thee to the Meeting for?

Lov.
To hear a Rascal hold forth for Bodkins and Thimbles, Contribution my beloved! to carry on the Good Cause, that is, Roguery, Rebellion, and Treason, prophaning the sacred Majesty of Heaven, and our glorious Sovereign.

Free.
But—were there not pretty. Women there?

Lov.
Damn 'em for sighing, groaning Hypocrites.

Free.
But there was one, whom, that handsom Face and Shape of yours, gave more occasion for sighing, than any Mortification caus'd by the Cant of the Lay Elder in the half Hogs Head; Did'st thou not mind her?

Lov.
Not I, damn it I was all Rage, and had'st not thou restrain'd me, I had certainly pull'd that Rogue of a Holder-forth by the Ears from his sanctify'd Tub. 'Sdeath he hum'd and haw'd all my Patience away, nose'd and snivel'd me to Madness. Heaven! That thou should'st suffer such Vermin to infect the Earth, such Wolves amongst thy Flocks, such Thieves and Robbers of all Laws of God and Man, in thy holy Temples. I rave to think to what thou'rt fall'n, poor *England*!

Free.
But the she Saint—

Lov.
No more, were she as fair as Fancy could imagine, to see her there,— wou'd make me loath the Form; she that can listen to the dull Non-

sence, the bantering of such a Rogue, such an illiterate Rascal, must be a Fool, past sense of loving, *Free-man.*

Free.
Thou art mistaken.—But, did'st thou mind her next the Pulpit?

Lov.
A Plague upon the whole Congregation: I minded nothing but how to fight the Lord's Battel with that damn'd sham Parson; whom I had a mind to beat.

Free.
My Lady *Desbro* is not of that Persuasion, but an errant Heroick in her Heart, and feigns it only to have the better occasion to serve the Royal Party. I knew her, and lov'd her before she married.

Lov.
She may chance then to be sav'd.

Free.
Come, I'll have thee bear up briskly to some one of 'em, it may redeem thy Sequestration; which, now thou see'st no hopes of compounding, puts thee out of Patience.

Lov.
Let 'em take it, and the Devil do 'em Good with it: I scorn it should be said I have a Foot of Land in this ungrateful and accursed Island; I'd rather beg where Laws are obey'd and Justice perform'd, than be powerful where Rogues and base born Rascals rule the Rost.

Free.
But suppose now, dear *Loveless*, that one of the Wives of these Pageant Lords should fall in love with thee, and get thy Estate again, or pay thee double for't?

Lov.
I wou'd refuse it.

Free.
And this for a little dissembled Love, a little Drudgery—

Lov.
Not a night by Heav'n—not an hour—no not a single kiss, I'd rather make love to an *Incubus*.

Free.
But suppose 'twere the new Protectoress her self, the fine Lady *Lambert*?

Lov.
The greatest Devil of all; Damn her, dost think I'll Cuckold the Ghost of old *Oliver*?

Free.
The better; there's some Revenge in't; do'st know her?

Lov.
Never saw her, nor care to do.

Cor.
Collonel, Do you command me any thing?

Free.
Yes, I'll send thee with a Note—Let's step into a Shop and write it; *Loveless* stay a moment, and I'll be with thee.

    [Ex. Free and Corporal.

    Enter L. Lambert, L. Desbro, Gilliflowr, Pages with great Bibles, and Footmen: Love. walks sullenly, not seeing 'em.

    [L. Lamb. Train carried.

La. Lam.
O, I'm impatient to know his Name; ah, *Desbro*, he betray'd all my Devotion; and when I wou'd have pray'd, Heav'n knows, it was to him, and for him onely.

The Roundheads; or, The Good Old Cause

L. *Des.*
What manner of man was it?

L. *Lam.*
I want words to describe him; not tall, nor short; well made, and such a face—Love, Wit, and Beauty revel'd in his Eyes:

From whence he shot a thousand winged Darts
That pierc'd quite through my Soul.

L. *Des.*
Seem'd he a Gentleman?

L. *Lam.*
A God! Altho his out-side were but mean; but he shone th'ro like Lightning from a Cloud, and shot more piercing Rayes.

L. *Des.*
Stay'd he long?

L. *Lam.*
No; methought he grew displeas'd with our Devotion
And seem'd to contradict the Parson with his Angry Eyes.
A Friend he had too with him, young and handsom,
Who seeing some disorder in his Actions, got him away.
—I had almost forgot all Decency,
And started up to call him, but my Quality
And wanting something to excuse that Fondness,
Made me decline with very much adoe.

Gill.
Heav'ns, Madam, I'll warrant they were Heroicks.

La. Lam.
Heroicks!

Gill.
Cavaliers, Madam, of the Royal Party.

L. D.
They were so, I knew one of 'em.

La. Lam.
Ah *Desbro*, do'st thou?
Ah Heav'ns, that they should prove Heroicks!

L. D.
You might have known that by the Conquest; I never heard, e're one o'th t'other Party ever gain'd a Heart: and indeed, Madam, 'tis a just Revenge, our Husbands make Slaves of them, and they kill all their Wives.

[Love, see 'em, and starts.

Lov.
Hah, what have we here?—Women—faith, and handsom too— I never saw a Form more Excellent! whoe're they are, they seem of Quality, —by Heav'n, I cannot take my Eyes from her.

[pointing to La. Lam.

La. Lam.
Hah, he's yonder, my Heart begins to fail,
My trembling Limbs refusing to support me—
His Eyes seem fix'd on mine too; ah, I faint—
[leans on Desbro.

Gill.
My Ladies Coach, *William*—quickly, she faints.

Lov.
Madam, can an unfortunate Stranger's aid add any thing to the recovery of so much Beauty?

[bowing, and holding her.

The Roundheads; or, The Good Old Cause

La. Lam.
Ah, Wou'd he knew how much!
       [*aside.*

Gill.
Support her, Sir, till her Ladiships Coach comes—I beseech ye.

Lov.
Not *Atlas* bore up Heaven with greater Pride.

La. Lam.
I beg your Pardon, Sir, for this Disorder
That has occasion'd you so great a Trouble—
You seem a Gentleman—and consequently
May need some Service done you; name the way,
I shall be glad to let you see my Gratitude.

Lov.
If there be ought in me, that merits this amazing Favour from you, I owe my thanks to Nature that indow'd me with something in my Face that spoke my Heart.

La. Lam.
Heav'n! how he looks and speaks—

       [*to Desbro, aside.*

L. *Des.*
Oh, these Heroicks, Madam, have the most charming Tongues.

La. Lam.
Pray come to me—and ask for any of my Officers, and you shall have admittance—

Lov.
Who shall I ask for Madam? for I'm yet ignorant to whom I owe for this great Bounty.

La. Lam.
Not know me! Thou art indeed a Stranger. I thought I'd been so Elevated above the common Crowd, it had been visible to all Eyes who I was.

Lov.
Pardon my Ignorance;
My Soul conceives ye all that Heaven can make ye,
Of Great, of Fair and Excellent;
But cannot guess a Name to call you by
But such as wou'd displease ye—
—[*aside.* My heart begins to fail, and by her Vanity
I fear she's one of the new Race of Quality:
—But be she Devil, I must love that Form.

La. Lam.
Hard Fate of Greatness, We so highly Elevated
Are more expos'd, to Censure than the little ones,
By being forc'd to speak our Passions first.
—Is my Coach ready?

Pag.
It waits your Honour.

La. Lam.

I give you leave to visit me—ask for the General's Lady, if my Title be not by that Time alter'd.

Lov.
Pistols and Daggers to my Heart—'tis so.

La. Lam.
Adiew Sir.

   Ex. all but Lov. who stands musing.

   Enter Freeman.

The Roundheads; or, The Good Old Cause

Free.
How now, what's the matter with thee?

Lov.
Prethee wake me *Freeman*.

Free.
Wake thee!

Lov.
I dream! by Heav'n I dream!
Nay yet the lovely Phantam's in my View,
Oh! wake me, or I sleep to perfect Madness.

Free.
What ayl'st thou, what did'st dream of?

Lov.
A strange fantastick Charmer,
A thing just like a Woman friend,
It walk't and look'd with wonderous Majesty,
Had Eyes that kill'd, and Graces deck'd her Face;
But when she talk'd, mad as the Winds she grew.
Chimera in the form of Angel, Woman!

Free.
Who the Devil meanest thou?

Lov.
By Heav'n I know not; but, as she vanish'd hence, she bad me come to th' General's!

Free.
Why this is she I told thee ey'd thee so at the Conventicle; 'tis *Lambert*, the renown'd, the famous Lady *Lambert*—Mad call'st thou her? 'tis her ill acted Greatness, thou mistak'st; thou art not us'd to the Pageantry of these Women yet; they all run thus mad: 'tis greatness in 'em, *Loveless*.

15

The Roundheads; or, The Good Old Cause

Lov.
And is thine thus, thy Lady *Desbro*?

Free.
She's of another Cut, she married as most do, for Interest,—but what—thou't to her?

Lov.
If Lightening stop my way,
Perhaps a sober view may make me hate her.
          Exit. both.

      Enter Lambert and Whitlock.

        Scen. A Chamber.

Whit.
My Lord, now is your time, you may be King; Fortune is yours, you've time itself by th' fore-lock.

Lam.
If I thought so, I'd hold him fast by Heaven.

Whit.
If you let slip this Opportunity, my Lord, you are undone— *Aut Cæsar, aut Nullus.*

Lam.
But *Fleetwood*—

Whit.
Hang him soft head.

Lam.
True, he's of an easie Nature, yet if thou did'st but know how little Wit governs this mighty Universe, thou wou'dst not wonder men should set up him.

The Roundheads; or, The Good Old Cause

Whit.
That will not recommend him at this *Juncto*, though he's an excellent Tool for your Lordship to make use of; and therefore, use him Sir as *Cataline* did *Lentulus*; drill the dull Fool with hopes of Empire, on, and that all tends to his Advancement only: The Block-head will believe the Crown his own: what other Hopes could make him ruine *Richard*, a Gentleman of Qualities a thousand times beyond him?

Lam.
They were both too soft; an ill Commendation for a General, who should be rough as storms of War it self.

Whit.
His Time was short, and yours is coming on; Old *Oliver* had his.

Lam.
I hate the Memory of that Tyrant *Oliver*.

Whit.
So do I, now he's dead, and serves my Ends no more. I lov'd the Father of the Great Heroick, whilst he had Power to do me good: he failing, Reason directed me to the Party then prevailing, the Fag End of the Parliament: 'tis true, I took the Oath of Allegiance, as *Oliver*, your Lordship, *Tony*, and the rest did, without which, we could not have sat in that Parliament; but that Oath was not for our Advantage, and so better broke than kept.

Lam.
I am of your Opinion my Lord.

Whit.
Let Honesty and Religion preach against it; but how cou'd I have serv'd the Commons by deserting the King? how have show'd my self loyal to your Interest, by fooling *Fleetwood*, in the deserting of *Dick*; by dissolving the honest Parliament, and bringing in the odious Rump? how cou'd I have flatter'd *Treton*, by telling him, Providence brought things about, when 'twas mere knavery all, and that the

hand of the Lord was in't, when I knew the Devil was in't? or indeed, how cou'd I now advise you to be King, if I had started at Oaths, or prefer'd Honesty or Divinity before Interest and the *Good Old Cause*.

Lam.
Nay, 'tis most certain, he that will live in this World, must be indu'd with the three rare Qualities of Dissimulation, Equivocation, and mental Reservation.

Whit.
In which Excellency, Heav'n be prais'd, we out-do the *Jesuits*.

Enter La. Lam.

L. *Lamb.*
I'm glad to see you so well employ'd my Lord, as in Discourse with my Lord *Whitlock* he's of our party, and has Wit.

Whit.
Your Honour graces me too much.

Lam.
My Lord, my Lady is an absolute States-Woman.

La. Lam.
Yes, I think things had not arriv'd to this exalted height, nor had you been in Prospect of a Crown, had not my Politicks exceeded your meaner Ambition.

Lam.
I confess, I owe all my good fortune to thee.

Enter Page.

Pag.
My Lord, my Lord *Wariston*, Lord *Hewson*, Collonel *Cobbet*, and Collonel *Duckenfield* desire the Honour of waiting on you.

The Roundheads; or, The Good Old Cause

La. Lam.
This has a Eace of Greatness—let 'em wait a while i'th' Antichamber.

Lam.
My Love, I wou'd have 'em come in.

La. Lam.
You wou'd have 'em, you wou'd have a Fools Head of your own; pray let me be Judge of what their Duty is, and what your Glory; I say I'll have 'em wait.

Page.
My Lord *Fleetwood* too is just alighted, shall he wait too Madam?

La. Lam.
He may approach; and d' ye hear—put on your fawning looks, flatter him, and profess much Friendship to him, you may betray him with the more facility.

Whit.
Madam, you counsel well,

[Ex. Page, re-enter with L. Fleetwood.

Enter Lord Fleetwood.

Lamb.
My good Lord, your most submissive Servant.

Whit.
My Gracious Lord, I am your Creature—your Slave—

Fleet.
I profess ingeniously, I am much ingag'd to you, my good Lords; I hope things are now in the Lard's handling, and will go on well for his Glory and my Interest, and that all my good People of *England* will do things that become good Christians.

Whit.
Doubt us not, my good Lord; the Government cannot be put into abler hands, than those of your Lordship; it has hitherto been in the hard clutches of *Jews*, *Infidels*, and *Pagans*.

Fleet.
Yea verily, Abomination has been in the hands of Iniquity.

Lam.
But, my Lord, those hands, by my good Conduct, are now cut off, and our Ambition is, your Lordship wou'd take the Government upon you.

Fleet.
I profess, my Lord, by ye and nay, I am asham'd of this Goodness, in making me the Instrument of saving Grace to this Nation; 'tis the great Work of the Lard.

La. Lam.
The Lard, Sir, I'll assure you the Lard has the least hand in your good fortune; I think you ought to ascribe it to the Cunning and Conduct of my Lord here, who so timely abandon'd the Interest of *Richard*.

Fleet.
Ingeniously, I must own, your good Lord can do much, and has done much; but 'tis our Method to ascribe all to the Powers above.

La. Lam.
Then I must tell you, your Method's an ungrateful Method.

Lam.
Peace, my Love.

Whit.
Madam, This is the Cant we must delude the Rabble with.

The Roundheads; or, The Good Old Cause

La. Lam.
Then let him use it there, my Lord, not amongst us, who so well understand one another.

Lam.
Good Dear, be pacifi'd—and tell me, shall the Gentlemen without have admittance?

La. Lam.
They may.

> [*Page goes out.*

> Enter *Hewson, Desbro, Duckenfield, Wariston* , and *Cobbet.*

War.
Guds Benizon light on yu, my gued Loords, for this days work; Madam, I kiss your white Honds.

Duc.
My Lord, I have not been behind hand in this days turn of State.

Lam.
'Tis confess'd, Sir; What wou'd you infer from that?

Duc.
Why, I wou'd know how things go; who shall be General, who Protector, or who King next.

Hews.
My Friend has well translated his meaning.

La. Lam.
Fy, how that filthy Cobler Lord betrayes his Function.

Duc.
We're in a Chaos, a Confusion, as we are.

The Roundheads; or, The Good Old Cause

Hews.
Indeed the Commonwealth at present is out at heels, and wants underlaying.

Cob.
And the People expect something suddenly from us.

Whit.
My Lords and Gentlemen, we must consider a while.

War.
Bread a gued there's mickle Wisdom i that Sirs.

Duc.
It ought to be consulted betimes, my Lord, 'tis a matter of moment, and ought to be consulted by the whole Committee.

Lam.
We design no other, my Lord, for which reason, at three a clock we'll meet at *Wallingford* House.

Duc.
Nay, my Lord, do but settle the Affair, let's but know who's our Head, and 'tis no matter.

Hew.
Ay, my Lord, no matter who; I hope 'twill be *Fleetwood*, for I have the length of his Foot already.

Whit.
You are the leading men, Gentlemen, your Voices will soon settle the Nation.

Duc.
Well, my Lord, we'll not fail at three a clock.

Des.
This falls out well for me; for I have Bus'ness in *Smithfield* , where my Horses stand; and verily, now I think on't, the Rogue the Ostler has

The Roundheads; or, The Good Old Cause

not given 'em Oates to day: Well, my Lords, farewel; if I come not time enough to *Wallingford* House, keep me a place in the Committee, and let my Voice stand for one, no matter who.

War.
A gued Mon I's warrant, and takes muckle Pains for the Gued o'th' Nation, and the Liberty o'th' Mobily:—The Diel confound 'em aud.

Lam.
Come, my Lord *Wariston*, you are a wise man, What Government are you for?

War.
Ene tol what ya please my gued Loord.

> [takes him aside.

Lam.
What think you of a single Person here in my Lord *Fleetwood*?

War.
Mary Sir, and he's a brave Mon, but gen I may cooncel, tak't for yar sel my gued Loord, ant be gued for him, 'tis ene gued for ya te.

Lam.
But above half the Nation are for him.

War.
Bread a gued, and I's for him than.

Fleet.
The Will of the Lard be done; and since 'tis his Will, I cannot withstand my Fate—ingeniously.

Whit.
My Lord *Wariston*, a Word—what if *Lambert* were the Man?

> [takes him aside.

War.
Right Sir, Wons and ya have spoken aud; He's a brave Mon, a Mon indeed gen I's 'ave any Judgment.

Whit.
So I find this Property's for any use.

        [*aside.*

Lam.
My Lord, I perceive Heaven and Earth conspire to make you our Prince.

Fleet.
Ingeniously, my Lords, the weight of three Kingdoms is a heavy Burden for so weak Parts as mine; therefore, I will, before I appear at Councel, go seek the Lard in this great Affair; and, if I receive a Revelation for it, I shall with all Humility espouse the Yoke, for the Good of his People and mine: and so Gad with us, the Commonwealth of *England*.

        Ex. Fleet. Desbro, Wariston, Duc. Cob. Hus. and Whit.

La. Lam.
Poor deluded Wretch, 'tis not yet come to that.

Lam.
No my Dear, the Voice will go clearly for me; what with Bribes to some, Hypocrisie and Pretence of Religion to others, and promis'd Preferments to the rest, I have engag'd 'em all.

La. Lam.
And will you be a King?

Lam.
You think that's so fine a thing—but let me tell you, my Love, a King's a Slave to a Protector, a King's ty'd up to a thousand Rules of musty Law, which we can break at Pleasure; we can rule without

The Roundheads; or, The Good Old Cause

Parliaments, at least, chuse whom we please, make 'em agree to our Proposals, or set a Guard upon 'em, and starve 'em till they do.

La. Lam.
But their Votes are the strangest things,—that they must pass for Laws; you were never voted King.

Lam.
No, nor care to be: the sharpest Sword's my Vote, My Law, my Title. They voted *Dick* should reign, where is he now? They voted the great Heroicks from the Succession; but had they Arms or Men, as I have, you shou'd soon see what wou'd become of their Votes—No my Love! 'Tis this —must make me King.

      [His Sword.

Let *Fleetwood* and the *Rump* go seek the Lard,
My Empire and my Trust is in my Sword.

ACT II.

Scene I.

A Chamber of State.

Enter *La. Lambert, Gilliflower, and Women-servants.*

La. Lam.
Gilliflower, Has none been here to ask for any of my People, in order to his approach to me?

Gill.
None, Madam.

La. Lam.
Madam! how dull thou art! wou't never learn to give me a better Title, than such an one as foolish Custom bestows on every common Wench?

Gill.
Pardon my Ignorance, Madam.

La. Lam.
Again Madam!

Gill.
Really, Madam, I shou'd be glad to know by what other Title you wou'd be distinguish'd?

La. Lam.
Abominable dull! Do'st thou not know on what score my Dear is gone to *Wallingford* House?

Gill.
I cannot divine, Madam.

The Roundheads; or, The Good Old Cause

La. Lam.
Heav'n help thy Ignorance! he's gone to be made Protector, fool, or at least, a King, thou Creature; And from this day I date my self her Highness.

Gill.
That will be very fine indeed, an't please your Highness.

La. Lam.
I think 'twill sute better with my Person and Beauty than with that other Woman—what d' ye call her? Mrs. *Cromwel*—my shape—and Gate—my Humour, and my Youth, have something more of Grandeur— have they not?

Gill.
Infinitely, an't please your Highness.

Enter Page.

Pag.
Madam, a Man without has the boldness to ask for your Honour.

La. Lam.
Honour, fool!

Gill.
Her Highness, Blockhead.

Pag.
Sawcily prest in, and struck the Porter for denying him entrance to your—Highness.

La. Lam.
What kind of Fellow was't?

Pag.
A rude, rough, Hectoring Swash, an't please your Highness; nay, and two or three times, Gad forgive me, he swore too.

The Roundheads; or, The Good Old Cause

La. Lam.
It must be he.

      [aside.

Pag.
His Habit was something bad and Cavalierish—I believe 'tis some poor petitioning, begging Tory, who having been sequester'd, wou'd press your Highness for some Favour.

La. Lam.
Yes, it must be he—ah foolish Creature! and can he hope Relief, and a villanous Cavalier? out upon 'em, poor Wretches—you may admit him tho', I long to hear how one of those things talk.

Gill.
Oh most strangely, Madam,—an't please your Highness, I shou'd say.

      Enter *Loveless.*

La. Lam.
'Tis he, I'll swear, *Gilliflower*, these Heroicks are punctual men,—how now, your Bus'ness with us, Fellow?

Lov.
My bus'ness, Madam?—

La. Lam.
Hast thou ever a Petition to us?

Lov.
A Petition, Madam?—Sure this put on Greatness is to amuse her Servants, or has she forgot that she invited me; or indeed forgot me?—

      [aside.

La. Lam.
What art thou?

Pag.
Shall we search his Breeches, an't please your Highness, for Pistol, or other Instruments?

La. Lam.
No Boy, we fear him not, they say the Pow'rs above protect the Persons of Princes.

[walks away.

Lov.
Sure she's mad, yet she walks loose about,
And she has Charms even in her Raving Fit.

La. Lam.
Answer me. What art thou? How shall I get my Servants hence with honour?

[aside.

Lov.
A Gentleman—
That cou'd have boasted Birth and Fortune too,
Till these accursed Times, which Heav'n confound,
Racing out all Nobility, all Vertue,
Has render'd me the rubbish of the World;
Whilst new rais'd Rascals, Canters, Robbers, Rebells
Do Lord it o're the Free-born, Brave and Noble.

La. La.
You're very confident, know you to whom you speak? but I suppose you have lost your Estate, or some such trivial thing, which makes you angry.

Lov.
Yes, a trivial Estate of some five and twenty hundred pound a year, but I hope to see that Rogue of a Lord reduc'd to his Cobler's Stall again, or, more deserv'dly hang'd, that has it.

The Roundheads; or, The Good Old Cause

La. Lam.
I thought 'twas some such Grievance—but you must keep a good Tongue in your head, lest you be hang'd for *Scandalum Magnatum* — there's Law for ye, Sir.

Lov.
No matter; then I shall be free from a damn'd Commonwealth, as you are pleas'd to call it, when indeed 'tis but a mungrel, mangy, Mock-Monarchy.

La. Lam.
Is it your bus'ness Sir to rail?

Lov.
You rais'd the Devil, Madam.

Pag.
Madam, shall I call your Highness Guards, and secure the Traytor?

La. La.
No; that you may see how little, I regard or fear him; leave us all—

[*Ex. all but Gill.*

We'll trust our Person in his hands alone—
—Now Sir—your Bus'ness?
[*smilingly approaches him.*

Lov.
Madam, I waited here by your Commands.

La. Lam.
How shall I tell him that I love him, *Gilliflower*?

Gill.
Easily, Madam, tell him so in plain *English*. Madam, 'tis great; Women of your exalted height ever speak first; you have no Equals dare pretend to speak of love to you.

The Roundheads; or, The Good Old Cause

La. Lam.
Thou art i'th' right—Do'st know my Quality, and thy own Poverty? And hast thou nothing to ask that I may grant?

Lov.
Sure she loves me! and I, frail flesh and blood,
Cannot resist her Charms; but she's of the damn'd Party.
        [*aside.*

La. Lam.
Are all your Party, Sir, so proud?

Lov.
But what have I to do with Religion? Is Beauty the worse, or a kind Wench to be refus'd for Conventickling? She lives high on the Spoils of a glorious Kingdom, and why may not I live upon the Sins of the Spoiler?

        [*aside.*

La. Lam.
Sir—you are poor!

Lov.
So is my Prince; a Plague on the occasion.

La. Lam.
I think you are—no Fool too?

Lov.
I wou'd I were, then I had been a Knave, had thriv'd, and possibly by this time had been tugging for rifled Crowns and Kingdoms.

La. Lam.
This Satyr ill befits my present Bus'ness with you,—you— want some Necessaries—as Cloaths, and Linnen too; and 'tis great pitty so proper a man shou'd want Necessaries. *Gilliflower*—take my Cabinet Key, and fetch the Purse of Broad-pieces that lyes in the lower

The Roundheads; or, The Good Old Cause

Drawer; 'tis a small Present, Sir, but 'tis an Earnest of my farther Service,

Gill. goes out, and returns with a Purse.

Lov.
I'm angry, that I find one Grain of Generosity in this whole Race of Hypocrites.

[*aside.*

La. Lam.
Here Sir, 'tis only for your present use; for Cloaths—three hundred Pieces; let me see you sweet—

Lov.
Stark mad, by this good day.

La. Lam.
Ah *Gilliflower*! How prettily those Cavalier things charm; I wonder how the Powers above came to give them all the Wit, Softness, and Gallantry,—whilst all the great ones of our Age have the most slovenly, ungrateful, dull Behaviour; no Ayr, no Wit, no Love, or any thing to please a Lady with.

Gill.
Truly Madam, there's a great Difference in the Men; yet Heav'n at first did it's part, but the Divel has since so over-done his, that what with the Vizor of Sanctity, which is the gadly Sneere, the drawing of the Face to a prodigious length, the formal language, with a certain Twang through the Nose, and the pious Gogle, they are fitter to scare Children than beget love in Ladies.

Lov.
You hit the Character of your new Saint.

La. Lam.
And then their Dress, *Gilliflower*.

The Roundheads; or, The Good Old Cause

Gill.
Oh! 'Tis an Abomination to look like a Gentleman; long Hair is wicked and Cavalierish, a Periwig is flat Popery, the Disguise of the Whore of *Babylon*; handsom Cloaths, or lac'd Linnen, the very Tempter himself, that debauches all their Wives and Daughters: therefore, the diminutive Band, with the Hair of the Reformation Cut, beneath which, a Pair of large sanctify'd Souses appear, to declare to the World, they had hitherto escap'd the Pillory, tho' deserv'd it as well as *Pryn*.

La. Lam.
Have a Care what you say, *Gilliflower*.

Gill.
Why Madam, we have no Informers here.

    Enter Page.

Page.
Madam, here's Old *Noll*'s Wife desires Admittance to your Hon— your Highness.

La. Lam.
Bid the poor Creature wait without, I'le do her what good I can for her Husbands sake, who first infus'd Politiques into me, by which I may boast I have clim'd to Empire.

Lov.
So, her Madness runs in that Vein I see.

    [*Aside.*

Gill.
Alack Madam, I think she's coming.

Crom. without.]
Does she keep state in the Divel's Name, and must I wait!

The Roundheads; or, The Good Old Cause

La. Lam.
Heav'ns! I shall be scandaliz'd by the godly, Dear *Gilliflower*, conceal my Cavalier; I wou'd not have a Cavalier seen with me for all the World.—Step into my Cabinet—

[Ex. Gill. and Lov.

Enter La. Cromwel, held back by a Man.—to them Gilliflower.

Crom.
Unhand me Villain—'twas not long since a Rudeness Sir like this had forfeited thy Head.

La. Lam.
What wou'd the Woman?

Crom.
The Knave, the perjur'd Villain thy Husband, byth' Throat, thou proud, imperious Baggage; to make me wait? who's Train thou hast been proud to bear—how durst thou, after an Affront like this, trust thy false Face within my Fingers reach? that Face, that first bewitch't the best of Husbands from me, and tempted him to sin.

Gill.
I beseech your Highness retire, the Woman's mad.

Cro.
Highness, in the Devil's name, sure 'tis not come to that; no, I may live to see thy Cuckold hang'd first, his Politicks are yet too shallow, Mistris. Heav'ns! Did my Husband make him Lord for this? raise him to Honour,

Trusts, Commands, and Councels,
To ruine all our Royal Family,
Betray'd young *Richard*, who had reign'd in Peace.
But for his Perjuries and Knaveries;
And now he sooths my Son in Law, soft *Fleetwood*,
With empty hopes of Pow'r, and all the while

The Roundheads; or, The Good Old Cause

To make himself a King:
No, Minion, no; I yet may live to see
Thy Husband's Head o'th top of *Westminster*
Before I see it circled in a Crown.

La. Lam.
I pity the poor Creature.

Crom.
Ungrateful Traytor as he is,
Not to look back upon his Benefactors;
But he, in lieu of making just Returns,
Reviles our Family, prophanes our Name,
And will in time render it far more odious
Than ever *Needham* made the great Heroicks.

La. Lam.
Alas, it weeps, poor Woman!

Cro.
Thou ly'st, false Strumpet, I scorn to shed a Tear
For ought that thou can'st do or say to me;
I've too much of my Husband's Spirit in me.
Oh, my dear *Richard*, had'st thou had a grain on't,
Thou and thy Mother ne'r had fall'n to this.

Gill.
His Father sure was seeking of the Lard when he was got.

Enter La. Fleetwood, her Train borne.

Crom.
Where is this perjur'd Slave, thy Wittal Lord?
Dares he not shew his Face, his guilty Face,
Before the Person he has thus betray'd?

L. Fleet.
Madam, I hope you mistake my honour'd Lord *Lambert*, I believe he designs the Throne for my dear Lord.

The Roundheads; or, The Good Old Cause

Crom.
Fond Girl, because he has the Art of fawning,
Dissembling to the height, can sooth and smile,
Profess, and sometimes weep:—
No, he will betray him, as he did thy Brother;
Richard the Fourth was thus deluded by him.
No, let him swear and promise what he will,
They are but Steps to his own ambitious End;
And only makes the Fool, thy credulous Husband
A silly deluded Property.

Enter Fleetwood.

Fleet.
My honour'd Mother, I am glad to find you here, I hope we shall reconcile things between ye. Verily, we shou'd live in brotherly Love together; come, ingeniously, you shall be Friends, my Lady Mother.

Cro.
Curse on th' occasion of thy being a Kin to me.

Flee.
Why, an please ye forsooth Madam?

Cro.
My Daughter had a Husband,
Worthy the Title of my Son in Law:
Ireton! my best of Sons: he'd Wit and Courage,
And with his Councels, rais'd our House to Honours,
Which thy impolitick Easiness pulls down:
And whilst you shou'd be gaining Crowns and Kingdoms
Art poorly couzening of the World with fruitless Prayers.

Fleet.
Nay, I'll warrant you Madam, when there is any gadly mischief to be done, I am as forward as the best, but 'tis good to take the Lard along with us in every thing. I profess ingeniously, as I am an honest man, verily— ne're stir—I shall act as becomes a good Christian.

The Roundheads; or, The Good Old Cause

Cro.
A Good Coxcombe.
Dost thou not see her reverend Highness there,
That Minion now assumes that glorious Title
I once, and my Son *Richard*'s Wife enjoy'd,
Whilst I am call'd the Night Mare of the Commonwealth?
But wou'd I were, I'd so hag-ride the perjur'd Slaves
Who took so many Oaths of true Allegiance
To my great Husband first, and then to *Richard*—
Who, whilst they reign'd, were most illustrious,
Most high and mighty Princes; whilst fawning Poets
Write Panegyricks on 'em: And yet no sooner was
The wonderous Heroe dead, but all his glorious
Titles fell to Monster of Mankind, Murderer
Of Piety, Traytor to Heav'n and Goodness.

Flee.
Who calls him so? Pray take their Names down: I profess ingeniously,
forsooth Madam, verily I'll order 'em, as I am here I will.

Cro.
Thou, alas they scorn so poor a thing as thou.

Fleet.
Do they ingeniously? I'll be even with 'em, forsooth Mother, as I am
here I will, and there's an end on't.

Cro.
I wou'd there were an end of our disgrace and shame, which is but
just begun, I fear.—

What will become of that fair Monument
Thy careful Father did erect for thee,
        [to La. Fleetw.

Yet whilst he liv'd, next to thy Husband *Ireton*?
Lest none shou'd do it for thee after he were dead?
The Malice of proud *Lambert* will destroy all.

The Roundheads; or, The Good Old Cause

Fleet.
I profess, Madam, you mistake my good Lord *Lambert*, he's an honest man, and fears the Lard; he tells me I am to be the man; verily he do's, after all's done.

Cro.
Yes, after all's done, thou art the man to be pointed at.

Fleet.
Nay, ingeniously, I scorn the words, so I do: I know the great Work of Salvation to the Nation is to be wrought by me, verily.

Cro.
Do, Cant on, till Heav'n drop Kingdoms in thy mouth: dull, silly Sot, thou ruine of our Interest: thou fond, inccorrigible, easie Fool.

Enter Page.

Pag.
My Lord, the Committee of Safety waits your coming.

Fleet.
Why, law you now, forsooth,—I profess verily, you are ingeniously the hardest of belief—tell the honourable Lords I'm coming: Go, Lady mother, go home with my Wife; and verily you'll see things go to your wish.—I must to Coach.—

L. Fleet.
Madam your humble Servant.
    [*to La. Lam.*

Fleet.
Honour'd Lady I kiss your hands.
        [*Ex. Crom. Fleet. and La. Fleet.*

Enter Loveless.

The Roundheads; or, The Good Old Cause

Lov.
Was this the thing that is to be Protector?
This little snivelling Fellow rule three Kingdoms?
But leave we Politicks, and fall to Love,
Who deals more Joyes in one kind, happy moment
Than Ages of Dull Empire can produce.

La. Lam.
Oh Gods! Shall I who never yielded yet,
But to him to whom three Kingdoms fell a Sacrifice,
Surrender at first Parly?

Lov.
Perhaps that Lover made ye gayer Presents,
But cou'd not render you a Heart all love,
Or mind embyass'd in Affairs of Blood.
—I bring no Guilt to fright ye from my Embraces,
But all our hours shall be serene and soft.

La. Lam.
Ah, *Gilliflower*, thy Aid, or I'm lost;
Shall it be said of me in after Ages
When my great Fame 'mongst Queens shall be recorded,
That I, ah Heav'ns! regardless of my Countries Cause,
Espous'd the wicked Party of its Enemies,
The Heathenish Heroicks! ah, defend me!

Lov.
Nay—by all that's—

La. Lam.
Ah hold! Do not prophane my Ears with Oaths or Execrations, I cannot bear the sound.

Lov.
Nay, nay,—by Heav'n I'll not depart your lodgings, till that soft Love that playes so in your Eyes give me a better proof—by—

La. Lam.
Oh hold, I dye, if you proceed in this Abomination!

Lov.
Why do you force me to't? d'ye think, to put me off with such a Face—such lips,—such smiles—such Eyes—and every Charm—You've made me mad, and I shall swear my Soul away, if disappointed now.

Gill.
Ah, save the Gentleman's Soul, I beseech ye, Madam.

La. Lam.
I'm much inclin'd to Acts of Piety—
> *leaning on him, smiling. He goes to lead her out,*
> *Enter La. Desbro.*

And you have such a Power, that howe're I incommode my Honour—
—*Desbro* here! how unseasonably she comes?

La. Des.
Cry mercy, Madam, I'll withdraw a while.

La. Lam.
Ah *Desbro*! thou art come—in the most lucky minute— I was just on the point of falling—As thou say'st, these Heroicks have the strangest Power—

La. Des.
I never knew a Woman cou'd resist 'em.

La. Lam.
No marvel then, our Husbands use 'em so, betray 'em, banish 'em, sequester, murder 'em, and every way disarm 'em.—

La. Des.
But their Eyes Madam.

La. Lam.
Ay, their Eyes *Desbro;* I wonder our Lords shou'd take away their Swords, and let 'em wear their Eyes.

La. Desbro.
I'll move it to the Committee of Safety, Madam, those Weapons shou'd be taken from 'em too.

La. Lam.
Still they'll have some to be reveng'd on us.

La. Des.
Ay, so they will; My Lord says, a *Cavalier* is a kind of *Hidra*, knock him o'th' Head as often as you will, he has still one to peep up withall.

      Enter Page.

Page.
Madam, here's Mr. *Freeman* to speak with your Honour.

Lov.
That's a Friend of mine Madam, and 'twou'd be unnecessary he saw your Highness and I together: let us withdraw—

La. Lam.
Withdraw, why, What will *Desbro* say?

Des.
O Madam, I know your Vertue and your Piety too well to suspect your Honour wrongfully? 'tis impossible a Lady that goes to a Conventicle twice a day, besides long Prayers and lowd Psalm-singing, shou'd do any thing with an Heroick against her Honour. Your known Sanctity preserves you from Scandal.—But here's *Freeman*—

      [Puts 'em in.

The Roundheads; or, The Good Old Cause

Enter Freeman.

Free.
So Madam—you are very kind—

La. Des.
My charming *Freeman*, this tedious day of Absence has been an Age in love! How hast thou liv'd without me?

Free.
Like one condemn'd, sad and disconsolate,
And all the while you made your Husband happy.

La. Des.
Name not the beastly Hypocrite, thou know'st
I make no other use of him,
But a dull Property to advance our Love.

Free.
And 'tis but *Justice, Maria*, he sequester'd me of my whole Estate, because, he said, I took up Arms in *Ireland*, on Noble *Ormond*'s Side; nay, hir'd Rogues, perjur'd Villains—Witnesses with a Pox, to swear it too; when at that Time, I was but eight years old: But I 'scapt as well as all the Gentry and Nobility of *England* . To add to this, he takes my Mistress too.

La. Des.
You mistake, my lovely *Freeman*; I marryed only thy Estate, the best Composition I cou'd make for thee, and I will pay it back with Interest too.

Free.
You wou'd suspect my love then, and swear that all the Adoration I pay you, were, as we do to Heaven, for Int'rest only.

La. Des.
How you mistake my love, but do so still, so you will let me give these—Proofs of it.

The Roundheads; or, The Good Old Cause

[Gives him Gold.

Free.
Thus like *Atlante*, you drop Gold in my Pursuit
To love, I may not over-take you:
What's this, to giving me one happy minute?
Take back your Gold, and give me currant love,
The Treasure of your Heart, not of your Purse, —
When shall we meet *Maria*?

La. Des.
You know my leasure Hours are when my honourable Lord is busied in Affairs of State, or at his Prayers; from which long-winded Exercise I have of late withdrawn my self: three Hours by the Clock he prays extempory, which is, for National and Houshold Blessings: for the first— 'tis to confound the Interest of the King, that the Lard wou'd deliver him, his Friends, Adherers and Allies, wheresoever scatter'd about the Face of the whole Earth, into the Clutches of the righteous: Press 'em good Lard, even as the Vintager doth the Grape in the Wine-Press, till the Waters, and gliding Chanels are made red with the Blood of the wicked.

[In a Tone.

Free.
And grant the faithful to be mighty, and to be strong in Persecution; and more especially, Ah! I beseech thee confound that malignant Tory *Freeman*—that he may never rise up in Judgment against thy Servant, who has taken from him his Estate, his Sustinance, and Bread; give him Grace of thy infinite Mercy, to hang himself, if thy People can find no zealous Witnesses to swear him to the Gallows legally. Ah, we have done very much for thee Lard, thou shoud'st consider us thy Flock, and we shou'd be as good to thee in another thing.

[In a Tone.

La. Des.
Thou hit'st the zealous Twang right; sure thou hast been acquainted with some of 'em.

Free.
Damn 'em, no; what honest Man wou'd keep 'em Company, where harmless Wit and Mirth's a Sin, laughing scandalous, and a merry Glav, Abomination.

La. Des.
Yes, if you drink Healths my wicked Brother; otherwise, to be silently drunk, to be as abusive and satyrical as you please, upon the Heroicks, is allowable—for laughing, indeed 'tis not so well; but the precise Sneere and Grin is lawful; no swearing indeed, but lying and dissimulation in abundance—I'll assure you, they drink as deep, and entertain themselves as well with this silent way of lewd Debauchery, as you with all your Wit and Mirth, your Healths to the Royal Family.

Free.
Nay, I confess, 'tis a great Pleasure to cheat the World.

La. Des.
'Tis Power, as divine *Hobs* calls it.

Free.
But what's all this to Love? Where shall we meet anon?

La. Des.
I'll tell you, that will please you as well.—Your Friend is within, with her Highness that shall be, if the Divel and her Husband's Politicks agree about the matter.

Free.
Ha, has my cautious Railer manag'd matters so sleyly?

La. Des.
No, No, the Matter was manag'd to his Hand: You see how Heav'n brings things about, for the Good of your Party; this Bus'ness will be worth him, at least a thousand pound a Year, or two, well manag'd.— But see, my Ladies Woman.

The Roundheads; or, The Good Old Cause

Gill.
Oh *Madam*, my Lord!

> *[Running cross the Stage into her Ladies Chamber.*

Free.
Death, how shall I bring my Friend off? He'll certainly be ruin'd.

> Enter *Gill. Lov.* and *La. Lam.*

Gill.
Madam, he's coming up.

Lov.
Madam, for my self I care not, but much concern'd for you.

> *La. Lam. takes two Papers out of her Pock. and gives 'em to Lov. and Free.*

La. Lam.
Here, take these two Petitions, each of you one,— Poor Fellows—you may be gone, your Petitions will not be granted.

> Enter Lambert.

Lam.
How now, my Dear, what Petitions?—Friends, what's your Bus'ness?

La. Lam.
'Tis enough we know their Business Love, we are sufficient to dispatch such Suters, I hope.

Lam.
Pardon me, my Dear, I thought no harm; but I saw you frown, and that made me concern'd.

La. Lam.
Frown! 'Twou'd make any Body frown, to hear the Impudence of Gentlemen, these *Cavaliers*;—wou'd you think it my Dear, if this

The Roundheads; or, The Good Old Cause

Fellow has not the Impudence to petition for the Thirds of his Estate again, so justly taken from him for bearing Arms for the Man?—

La Des.
Nay, I am inform'd, that they, but two Nights ago, in a Tavern, Drunk a Health to the Man too.

Lam.
How durst you, Sirrah, approach my Lady with any such sawcy Address, you have receiv'd our Answer.

Lov.
Death, I've scarce Patience.

[*Aside.*

Free.
We knew, my Lord, the Influence your Ladies have over you, and Women are more tender and compassionate naturally, than Men; and Sir, 'tis hard for Gentlemen to starve.

La. Lam.
Have you not able Limbs, can ye not work—

Lov.
Persons of our Education work!

Lam.
Starve or beg then.

La. Lam.
Education, why, I'll warrant there was that young Creature they call the Duke of *Glocester*, was as well educated as any Lad in the Parish, and yet you see he should have been bound Prentice to a handy Crafts Trade, but that our Lords cou'd not spare Money to bind him out, and so they sent him to beg beyond Sea.

Lov.
Death, I shall do Mischief: not all the Joy she gave me but now, can attone for this Blasphemy against the Royal Youth.

The Roundheads; or, The Good Old Cause

Free.
Patience—Well my Lord, we find you are obdurate, and we'll withdraw.

Lam.
Do so: And if you dare presume to trouble us any more, I'll have you whip'd, d'e hear.

La. Des.
Madam, I'll take my leave of your Ladiship.

[*Ex. Lov. Free. & L. Des.*

La. Lam.
My Lord, 'twas I that ought to threaten 'em—but you'r so forward still—what makes you from the Committee?

Lam.
I left some Papers behind.

La. Lam.
And they'll make use of your Absence to set up *Fleetwood* King.

Lam.
I'll warrant ye my Dear.

La. Lam.
You'll warrant? you're a Fool and a Coxcomb; I see I must go my self, there will be no bus'ness done 'till I thunder 'em together: They want *Old Oliver* amongst 'em, his arbitrary Nod cou'd make ye all tremble; when he wanted Power or Money, he need but Cock in Parliament, and lay his hand upon his Sword, and cry, I must have Money, and had it, or kick'd ye all out a doors: And you are so mealy mouth'd, you cannot Cock for a Kingdom.

Lam.
I'll warrant you Dear, I can do as good a thing for a Kingdom.

La. Lam.
You can do nothing as you shou'd do't: You want Old *Oliver*'s Brains, Old *Oliver*'s Courage, and Old *Oliver*'s Counsel: Ah, what a politick Fellow was little Sir *Anthony*! What a Head-peice was there! What a plaguy Fellow Old *Thurlo*, and the rest: But get ye back, and return me Protector at least, or never hope for Peace again.

Lam.
My Soul trouble not thy self, go in—

With mine, no Power can equal be,
And I will be a King to humour thee.
   Exeunt.

The Roundheads; or, The Good Old Cause

ACT III.

Scene I.

A Council Chamber, great Table, Chairs, and Papers.

Enter two Clarks, who lay Papers in Order, and Door-keeper.

Door.
Come, Haste, Haste, the Lords are coming;—keep back there, room for the Lords, room for the honourable Lords: Heav'n bless your Worships Honours.

> Enter *Lambert, Fleetwood, Whitlock, Wariston, discoursing earnestly; to them Duckenfield, Cobbet, Hewson, Desbro, and others; Duck. takes Wariston by the Hand,* and *talks to him* .

War.
Bread a gued Gentlemen, I's serv'd the Commonwealth long and faithfully; I's turn'd and turn'd to aud Interest and aud Religions that turn'd up Trump, and wons a me, but I's get naught but Bagery by my Sol; I's noo put in for a Pansion as well as rest o ya Loones.

Cob.
What we can serve you in my Lord, you may command.

Duc.
And I too my Lord, when the Government is new moulded.

War.
Wons Sirs, and I's sa moold it; 'twas ne're sa moolded sin the Dam boond the Head on't.

Duc.
I know there are some ambitious Spirits that are for a single Person; but we'll have hot work e're yield to that.

The Roundheads; or, The Good Old Cause

War.
The faud Diel take 'em then for *Archibald*; 'tis warse than Monarchy.

Duc.
A thousand Times: Have we with such Industry, been pulling down Kings of the Royal Family, to set up Tyrants of our own, of mean and obscure Birth? No, if we're for a single Person, I'm for a lawful one.

War.
Wons and ya have spoken aud my Lord, so am I.

Duc.
But *Lambert* has a busie, haughty Spirit, and thinks to carry it; but we'll have no single Person.

War.
Nor I, ods Bread; the faud Diel brest the Wem of *Lambert*, or any single Person in *England*. I's for yare Interest my gued Lords.

[*Bowing.*

Lam.
My Lord *Wariston*, will you please to assume the Chair.

Enter *Loveless, Freeman, and others with Petitions.*

War.
Ah, my gued Loord, I's yare most obedient humble Servant.

[*Bowing to Lam. all set.*

All.
Hum, Hum.

Fleet.
My Lords and Gentlemen, we are here met together in the Name of the Lard—

The Roundheads; or, The Good Old Cause

Duc.
Yea, and I hope we shall hang together as one man.—A Pox upon your preaching.

    [Aside.

Fleet.
—And hope this days great work will be for his Praise and Glory.

Duc.
'Bating long Graces my Lord, we are met together for the Bus'ness of the Nation, to settle it, and to establish a Government.

Fleet.
Yea, verily: And I hope you will all unanimously agree, it shall be your unworthy Servant.

Lam.
What else my Lord?

Flee.
And as thou Lard has put the Sword into my hand—

Duc.
So put it into your Heart—My Lord, to do Justice.

Fleet.
Amen.

Duc.
I'd rather see it there than in your Hand.

    [Aside.

Fleet.
For, we are, as it were, a Body without a Head; or, to speak more learnedly, an Animal, unanimate.

The Roundheads; or, The Good Old Cause

Hus.
My Lord, let us use, as little as we can, the language of the Beast; hard Words, none of your Eloquence, it savoureth of Monarchy.

Lam.
My Lord, you must give men of Quality leave to speak in a Language more Gentile and Courtly than the ordinary sort of mankind.

Hew.
My Lord, I am sorry to hear there are any of Quality amongst this Honourable Dissembly.

    [stands up.

Cob.
Assembly, my Lord—

Hews.
Well, you know my meaning; or if there be any such, I'm sorry they shou'd own themselves of Quality.

Duc.
How, own themselves Gentlemen? Death Sir, d' ye think we were all born Coblers?

Hews.
Or if you were not, the more the pitty, for little *England*, I say.

    [in heat.

Fleet.
Verily, my Lords, Brethren shou'd not fall out, it is a scandal to the Good Cause, and maketh the Wicked rejoyce.

War.
Wons and theys garr the Loosey Proverb on't te, When Loons gang together by th' Luggs, gued men get their ene.

The Roundheads; or, The Good Old Cause

All.
He, he, he.

Duc.
He calls you Knaves by craft, my Lords.

War.
Bread a gued, tak't among yee Gentlemen, I's ment weele.

Fleet.
I profess, my Lord *Wariston*, you make my hair stand an end to hear how you swear.

War.
Wons, my Loord, I's sware as little as your Lordship, only I's sware out, and ya swallow aud.

Duc.
There's a Bone for you to pick, my Lord.

All.
He, he, he.

Lam.
We give my Lord *Wariston* leave to jest.

Des.
But what's this to the Government all this while? a dad I shall sit so late, I shall have no time to visit my Horses, therefore proceed to the Point.

Hews.
Ay, to the Point, my Lords; the Gentleman that spoke last spoke wll.

Cob.
Well sed Brother, I see you will in time speak properly.

The Roundheads; or, The Good Old Cause

Duc.
But to the Government, my Lords?

[*beats the Table.*

Lam.
Put 'em off o' this Discourse, my Lord.

[*aside to War.*

Des.
My Lord Wariston, move it, you are Speaker.

War.
The Diel a me, Sirs, and noo ya talk of a Speaker, I's tell ye a blithe Tale.

Fleet.
Ingeniously my Lord, you are to blame to swear so.

Lam.
Your Story, my Lord.

War.
By my Sol mon, and there was a poor Woman the other day beg'd ot'h' Carle the Speaker, but he'd give her nought unlas she'd lat a feart; wons at last a feart she lat, Ay marry, quoth the woman, noo my Rump has a Speaker te.

All.
He, he, he.

Duc.
But to our Bus'ness—

Des.
Bus'ness; ay, there's the thing, I've a world on't. I shou'd go and bespeak a pair of Mittens and Shears for my Hedger and Shearer, a

The Roundheads; or, The Good Old Cause

pair of Cards for my Thrasher, a Sythe for my Mower, and a Skreen-fan for my Lady Wife, and many other things; my Head's full of bus'ness—I cannot stay.—

Whit.
Fy my Lord, will you neglect the bus'ness o'th' day? we meet to oblige the Nation, and gratifie our Friends.

Des.
Nay, I'll do any thing, so I may rise time enough to see my Horses at night.

Lov.
Damn 'em, what stuff's here for a Council-Table?

Free.
Where are our English Spirits, that can be govern'd by such Dogs as these?—

Lam.
Clark, Read the Heads of what past at our last sitting.

War.
In the first place, I must mind your Lordships tol consider those that have been gued Members in the Commonwealth.

Fleet.
We shall not be backward to gratifie any that have serv'd the Commonwealth.

Whit.
There's Money enough; we have taxt the Nation high.

Duc.
Yes, if we knew where to find it: however read.

Clark reads.]
To *Walter Walton* Draper, six thousand nine hundred twenty nine pounds six shillings and five pence, for Blacks for his Highness Funeral.

The Roundheads; or, The Good Old Cause

Lam.
For the Devil's, put it down for *Oliver Cromwel*'s Funeral: We'll have no Records rise up in Judgment for such a Villain.

Lov.
How the live Asses kick the dead Lion?

[*aside.*

Duc.
Hark ye, my Lords, We sit here to reward Services done to the Commonwealth; let us consider whether this be a Service to the Commonwealth or not?

Lam.
However, we'll give him Paper for't.

Hews.
Ay, let him get his money when he can.

Lam.
Paper's not so dear, and the Clerk's pains will be rewarded.

War.
Right, my gued Loord, 'sbred, that *Cromwel* was th' faudest limmer Loon that ever cam intol our Country, the faud Diel has tane him by th' luggs for robbing our Houses and Land.

Fleet.
No swearing, my Lord.

War.
Weel, weel, my Loord, I's larne to profess and lee as weel as best on ya.

Hews.
That may bring you profit, my Lord—but Clerk proceed.

The Roundheads; or, The Good Old Cause

Clerk reads.]
To *Walter Frost*, Treasurer of the Contingencies, twenty thousand pounds: to *Thurloe*, Secretary to his Highness—

Duc.
To old *Nol.*—

Clerk reads]
Old *Nol*, ten thousand pound, for unknown Service done the Commonwealth—to Mr. *Hutchinson* Treasurer of the Navy, two hundred thousand pounds—

War.
Two hundred thousand pound; Owns what a Sum's there?—Marry it came from the Mouth of a Cannon sure.

Clerk reads.]
A Present to the Right Honourable and truly Vertuous Lady, the Lady *Lambert*, for Service done the late Protector.

Hews.
Again—say *Cromwel*.

Cler.
—*Cromwel*—six thousand pound in *Jacobus*'s.

War.
'Sbread, sike a Sum wou'd make me honour the face of aud *Jemmy* .

Clerk.
To Mr. *Ice* six thousand pound; to Mr. *Loether* late Secretary to his High—

Whit.
To *Oliver Cromwel* say, can you not obey Orders?

The Roundheads; or, The Good Old Cause

Cler.
—Secretary to *Oliver Cromwel*—two thousand nine hundred ninety nine pounds, for Intelligence and Information, and piously betraying the King's Liege People.

War.
Haud, haud Sirs, Mary en ya gift se fast ya'll gif aud away fro poor *Archibauld Johnson*.

Whit.
Speak for your self, my Lord; or rather my Lord, do you speak for him.

[to Lam

Lam.
Do you move it for him, and I'll do as much for you anon.

[aside to Whit.

Whit.
My Lord, since we are upon Gratifications,—let us consider the known Merits of the Lord *Wareston*, a Person of industrious mischiefs to the Malignant Party, and great Integrity to us, and the Commonwealth.

War.
Gued faith an I's ha been a trusty Trojon Sirs, what say you my very gued and gracious Loords?—

Duc.
I scorn to let a Dog go unrewarded; and you, Sir, fawn so prettily, 'tis pity you shou'd miss Preferment.

Hews.
And so 'tis; come, come, my Lords, consider he was ever our Friend, and 'tis but reasonable we shou'd stich up one another's broken Fortunes.

The Roundheads; or, The Good Old Cause

Duc.
Nay Sir, I'm not against it.

All.
'Tis reason, 'tis reason.

Free.
Damn 'em, how they lavish out the Nation?

War.
Scribe, pretha read my Paper—

Hews.
Have you a pertition there!

Cob.
A Pitition, my Lord.

Hews.
Pshaw, You Scholards are so troublesom.

Lam.
Read the Substance of it.

[*to the Clerk.*

Cler.
That your Honours wou'd be pleas'd, in consideration of his Services, to grant to your Petitioner a considerable Sum of Money for his present supply.

Fleet.
Verily, order him two thousand pound—

War.
Two thousand poond? Bread a gued, and I's gif my Voice for Fleetwood.

[*aside.*

59

The Roundheads; or, The Good Old Cause

Lam.
Two thousand; nay, my Lords, let it be three.

War.
Wons, I lee'd, I leed; I's keep my Voice for *Lambert*. —gueds Benizon light on yar Sol, my gued Lord *Lambert*.

Hews.
Three thousand pound, why such a Sum wou'd buy half *Scotland*.

War.
Wons, my Lord, ya look but blindly on't then: time was, a mite on't had bought and shoos in yar Stall, Brother, tho' noo ya so abound in Irish and Bishops Lands.

Duc.
You have nick'd him there, my Lord.

All.
He, he, he.

War.
Scribe—gang a tiny bit farther.

Clerk.
—And that your Honours wou'd be pleas'd to confer an Annual Pension on him.—

Lam.
Reason, I think; What say you my Lords of five hundred pound a year?

All.
Agreed, agreed.

War.
The Diel swallow me, my Lord, ya won my heart.

The Roundheads; or, The Good Old Cause

Duc.
'Tis very well—but out of what shall this be rais'd?

Lam.
We'll look what Malignants Estates are forfeit, undispos'd of— let me see—who has young *Freeman*'s Estate?

Des.
My Lord, that fell to me.

Lam.
What all the fifteen hundred pound a year?

Des.
A dad, and all little enough.

Free.
The Devil do him good with it.

Des.
Had not the Lard put it into your hearts to have given me two thousand *par an um* out of Bishops Lands, and three thousand *par an um* out of the Marquess's Estate; how shou'd I have liv'd and serv'd the Commonwealth as I have done?

Free.
A plague confound his Honour, he makes a hard shift to live on Eight thousand pound a year, who was born and bred a Hedger.

Lov.
Patience, Friend.

Lam.
I have been thinking—but I'll find out a way.

Lov.
Or betray some honest Gentleman, on purpose to gratifie the Loone.

The Roundheads; or, The Good Old Cause

Lam.
And Gentlemen, I am bound in Honour and Conscience to speak in behalf of my Lord *Whitlock*; I think fit, if you agree with me, he shou'd be made Constable of *Windsor* Castle, Warden of the Forrest, with the Rents, Perquisites, and Profits thereto belonging, nor can your Lordships confer a Place of greater Trust and Honour in more safe hands.

Duc.
I find he wou'd oblige all to his side.
             [*aside.*
Has he not part of the Duke of *Buckingham*'s Estate already, with *Chelsey* House, and several other Gifts?

Lam.
He has dearly deserv'd 'em, he has serv'd our Interest well and faithfully.

Duc.
And he has been well paid for't.

Whit.
And so were you, Sir, with several Lordships, and Bishops Lands, you were not born to, I conceive.

Duc.
I have not got it, Sir, by Knavish Querks in Law, a Sword that deals out Kingdoms to the brave, has cut out some small parcels of Earth for me, And what of this?

             [*stands up in a heat.*

Whit
I think, Sir, he that talks well, and to'th purpose, may be as useful to the Commonwealth as he that fights well; Why do we keep so many else in Pension that ne'r drew Sword, but to talk, and rail at the

The Roundheads; or, The Good Old Cause

Malignant Party; to libel and defame 'em handsomly, with pious, useful Lyes:

Which pass for Gospel with the common Rabble,
And Edifie more than *Hugh Peters*'s Sermons?
And make Fools bring more Grist to th' publick Mill:
Then Sir—to wrest the Law to our convenience
Is no small, inconsiderate Work?

Free.
And which you may be hang'd for very shortly—
            [*aside.*

Lam.
'Tis granted, my Lord, your Merit's infinite,—
We made him Keeper of the Great Seal, 'tis true, 'tis Honour, but no Salary.

Duc.
Ten thousand pound a year in Bribes will do as well.

Lam.
Bribes are not so frequent now as in Old *Noll*'s dayes.

Hews.
Well, my Lord, let us be brief and tedious, as the saying as, and humour one another; I'm for *Whitlock*'s advance.

Lam.
I move for a Salary, Gentlemen, *Scobel* and other petty Clerks have had a thousand a year, my Lord sure merits more.

Hews.
Why,—let him have two thousand then.

The Roundheads; or, The Good Old Cause

Flee.
I profess ingeniously, with all my heart.

Whit.
I humbly thank your Lordships—but, if I may be so bold to ask, from whence shall I receive it?

Lam.
Out of the Customs.

Cob.
Brotherly love ought to go along with us—but, under favour, when this is gone, where shall we raise new supplies?

Lam.
We'll tax the Nation high, the City higher;
They are our Friends, our most obsequious Slaves,
Our Dogs, to fetch and carry, our very Asses—

Lov.
And our Oxes, with the help of their Wives.
        [aside.

Lam.
Besides, the City's rich, and near her time, I hope, of being deliver'd.

War.
Wons a gued, wad I'd the laying o her, she shou'd be sweetly brought to Bed, by my Sol.

Des.
The City cares for no *Scotch* Pipers, my Lord.

War.
By my Sol, but she has danc'd after the gued Pipe of Reformation, when the Covenant Jigg gang'd maryly round Sirs.

Cla.
My Lords, here are some poor malignant Petitioners.

The Roundheads; or, The Good Old Cause

Lam.
Oh, turn 'em out, here's nothing for 'em; these Fellows were petitioning my Lady to day—I thought she had given you a satisfactory Answer?

Lov.
She did indeed, my Lord; but, 'tis a hard Case, to take away a Gentleman's Estate, without convicting him of any Crime.

Lam.
Oh Sir! we shall prove that hereafter.

Lov.
But to make sure Work, you'll hang a man first, and examine his Offence afterwards; a Plague upon your Consciences: my Friend here had a little fairer Play, your Villains, your Witnesses in Pension swore him a Collonel for our Glorious Master, of ever blessed Memory, at eight years old; a Plague upon their miracles.

Fleet.
Ingeniously, Sirrah, you shall be pillory'd for defaming our reverend Witnesses: Guards take 'em to your Custody both.

Free.
Damn it, I shall miss my Assignation with Lady *Desbro*; a Pox of your unnecessary Prating, what shall I do?

    [Guards take 'em away.

Lam.
And now, my Lords, we have finish'd the bus'ness of the Day. My good Lord *Fleetwood*, I am entirely yours, and at our next sitting shall approve my self your Creature.—

Whit.
My good Lord, I am your submissive Vassal.

Wariston.
Wons my Lord, I scorn any man shou'd be mere yare Vassal than *Archibald Johnson.*

[To Fleetwood.

Ex. All.

Scene II

SCENE. A Chamber.

Enter La. Desbro. and Corporal in haste.

La. Des.
Seiz'd on, secur'd, was there no time but this? What made him at the Committee, or when there, why spoke he honest Truth? What shall I do, good Corporal Advise: take Gold, and see if you can corrupt his Guards, but they are better paid for doing mischief; yet try, their Consciences are large.

[Gives him Gold.

Cor.
I'll venture my Life in so good a Cause, *Madam.*

Ex.

Enter Page.

Pag.
Madam here's *Mr. Ananias Gogle,* the Lay Elder of *Clements* Parish.

La. Des.
Dam the sham Saint; am I now in Condition to be plagu'd with his impertinent Non-sense?

Pag.
Oh! Pray Madam hear him preach a little; 'tis the purest sport.—

The Roundheads; or, The Good Old Cause

Enter *Ananias*.

Ana.
Peace be in this Place.

La. Des.
A blessed Hearing; he preaches nothing on his Conventicles, but Blood and Slaughter.
        [Aside.
What wou'd you Sir, I'm something busie now.

Ana.
Ah, the Children of the Elect have no Business, but the great work of Reformation? Yea verily, I say, all other Business is prophane, and diabolical, and divelish; Yea, I say, these Dressings, Curles, and shining Habilliments,—which take so up your time, your precious time; I say, they are an Abomination, yea, an Abomination in the sight of the Righteous, and serve but as an *Ignis fatuus*, to lead vain man astray.—I say again—

      [Looking now and then behind on the Page.

La. Des.
—You are a very Coxcomb.

Ana.
I say again, that even I, upright I, one of the new Saints, find a sort of a—a—a—I know not what,—a kind of a—Motion as it were— a stirring up—as a man may say, to Wickedness;—Yea, verily it corrupteth the outward man within me.

La. Des.
Is this your Business Sir, to rail against my Cloaths, as if you intended to preach me into my Primitive Nakedness again?

Ana.
Ah, the Naked Truth is best; but, *Madam*, I have a little work of Grace to communicate unto you, please you to send your Page away—

The Roundheads; or, The Good Old Cause

La. Des.
Withdraw—sure I can make my Party good with one wicked Elder: Now Sir—your Bus'ness.

Ex. Page.

—Be brief.

Ana.
As brief as you please—but—who in the sight of so much Beau—ty— can think of any Bus'ness but the Bus'ness!—Ah! hide those tempting Breasts,— Alack, how smoth and warm they are—

[Feeling 'em, and sneering.

La. Des.
How now, Have you forgot your Function?

Ana.
Nay, but I am mortal man also, and may fall seven times a day;— Yea verily, I may fall seven times a day:—Your Ladiships Husband is old,—and where there is a good Excuse for falling,—Ah, there the fall-ing— is excusable.—And might I but fall with your Ladiship,— might I, I say.—

La. Des.
How, this from you, the Head o'th' Church militant; the very Pope of Presbytery?

Ana.
Verily, the Sin lyeth in the Scandal; therefore, most of the discreet pious Ladies of the Age, chuse us, upright men, who make a Conscienee of a secret, the Laiety being more regardless of their Fame.—In sober sadness, the Place—inviteth, the Creature tempting, and the Spirit very violent within me.

[Takes and ruffles her.

The Roundheads; or, The Good Old Cause

L. Des.
Who waits there?—I'm glad you have prov'd your self what I ever thought of all your pack of Knaves.

An,
Ah, Madam! Do not ruine my Reputation; there are Ladies of high Degree in the Commonwealth, to whom we find our selves most comforting; why might not you be one?—for, alas, we are accounted as able men in Ladies Chambers, as in our Pulpits; we serve both Functions—

Enter Servants.

Hah! her Servants—
       [*stands at a distance.*

La. Des.
Shou'd I tell this, I shou'd not find belief.

       [*aside.*

Anan.
Madam, I have another Errand to your Ladiship.—It is the Duty of my Occupation to catechize the Heads of every Family within my Diocese; and you must answer some few Questions I shall ask—In the first place, Madam—Who made ye?

La. Des.
So, from whoring to a zealous Catechism—who made me? what Insolence is this, to ask me Questions which every Child that lisps out words can answer.

An.
'Tis our Method, Madam.

La. Des.
Your Impudence Sirrah—let me examine your Faith, who are so sawcy to take an account of mine—Who made you? But lest you

The Roundheads; or, The Good Old Cause

shou'd not know, I will inform you: First, Heav'n made you a deform'd, ill favour'd Creature, then the Rascal your Father made you a Taylor, next, your Wife made you a Cuckold, aud lastly, the Devil has made you a Doctor: and so get you gone for a Fool and a Knave all over.

Ana.
A man of my Coat affronted thus!

La. Des.
It shall be worse, Sirrah, my Husband shall know how kind you wou'd have been to him, because your Disciple and Benefactor, to have begot him a Babe of Grace for a Son and Heir.

Ana.
Mistake not my pious meaning, most Gracious Lady.

La. Des.
I'll set you out in your Colours: your impudent and Bloody Principles, your cheats, your Rogueries on honest men, through their kind, deluded Wives, whom you cant and goggle into a Belief, 'tis a great work of Grace to steal, and beggar their whole Families, to contribute to your Gormandizing, Lust, and Laziness; Ye Locusts of the Land, preach Nonsence, Blasphemy, and Treason, till you sweat again, that the Sanctifi'd Sisters my rub you down, to comfort and console the Creature.

Ana.
Ah! Am—

La. Des.
Sirrah, be gone, and trouble me no more—be gone—yet stay— the Rogue may be of Use to me—amongst the heap of Vice, Hypocrisie, and Devils that possess all your Party, you may have some necessary sin; I've known some honest, useful Villains amongst you, that will swear, profess, and lie devoutly for the Good Old Cause.

The Roundheads; or, The Good Old Cause

Ana.
Yea verily, I hope there are many such, and I shou'd rejoyce, yea, exceedingly rejoyce, in any Gadly Performance to your Ladiship.

La. Des.
This is a pious Work: You are a Knave of Credit, a very Saint with the rascally Rabble, with whom your Seditious Cant more prevails, your precious hum and ha, and gifted Nonsense, than all the Rhetorick of the learn'd or honest.

Ana.
Hah!

La. Des.
—In fine, I have use of your Talent at present, there's one now in Confinement of the Royal Party—his name's *Freeman*.

Ana.
And your Ladiship wou'd have him dispatch'd; I conceive ye— but wou'd you have him dispatch'd privately, or by Form of Law? we've Tools for all uses, and 'tis a pious Work and meritorious.

La. Des.
Right: I wou'd indeed have him dispatch'd, and privately; but 'tis hither privately, hither, to my Chamber, privately, for I have private Bus'ness with him: D' ye start?—this must be done—for you can pimp I'm sure upon occasion, you've Tools for all uses; come, resolve, or I'll discover your bloody offer; Is your Stomach so queasie it cannot digest Pimping, that can swallow Whoring, false Oaths, Sequestration, Robbery, Rapes, and Murders daily?

Ana.
Verily, you mistake my pious meaning; it is the Malignant I stick at; the Person, not the Office: and in sadness, Madam, it goeth against my tender Conscience to do any good to one of the Wicked.

La. Des.
It must stretch at this time; go haste to the Guard, and demand him in my Husband's Name; here's something worth your Pains—

having releas'd him, bring him to me, you understand me—go bid him be diligent, and as you behave your self, find my Favour; for know, Sir, I am as great an Hypocrite as you, and know the Cheats of your Religion too; and since we know one another, 'tis like we shall be true.

Ana.
But shou'd the man be missing, and I call'd to an account?—

La. Des.
He shall be return'd in an hour; go, get you gon, and bring him, or—no more—

Ex. Ana.

For all degrees of Vices, you must grant
There is no Rogue like your *Geneva* Saint.

ACT IV.

Scene I.

Chamber, Candles and Lights.

Enter La. Desbro, and Freeman.

La. Des.
By what strange Miracle, my dearest *Freeman*, wert thou set at Liberty?

Free.
On the zealous Parole of *Rabbie Ananias*; that Rhetorick that can convert whole Congregations of well-meaning Block-heads, to errant Knaves, has now mollify'd my Keeper; I'm to be render'd back within this Hour: let's not, my dear *Maria*, lose the precious minutes this Reverend Hypocrite has given us.

La. Des.
Oh! You are very gay, have you forgot whose Prisoner you are, and that perhaps, e're many days are ended, they may hang you for High Treason against the Common-wealth? they never want good throw-stitch'd Witness, to do a Murder lawfully.

Free.
No matter; then I shall dye with Joy, *Maria*, when I consider, that you lov'd so well to give me the last Proof on't.

La. Des.
Are you in Earnest, *Freeman*, and wou'd you take what Honour will not suffer me to grant?

Free.
With all my Heart, Honour's a poor Excuse: Your Heart and Vows (your better part) are mine; you've only lent your Body out to one whom you call Husband, and whom Heav'n has mark'd for Cuckoldom. Nay, 'tis an Act of honest Loyalty, so to revenge our

The Roundheads; or, The Good Old Cause

Cause; whilst you were only mine, my honest Love thought it a Sin to press these Favours from you; 'twas injuring my self as well as thee; But now we only give and take our Right.

La. Des.
No more, my Husband's old.—

Free.
Right my Dear *Maria*;—and therefore,—

La. Des.
—May possibly dye.—

Free.
He will be hang'd first.

La. Des.
—I hope so—either of which, will do our Business:— Unreasonable *Freeman*, not to have Patience till my Husband be hang'd a little.

Free.
But what if Destiny put the Change upon us, and I be hang'd instead of *Desbro*?

La. Des.
Why then thou art not the first Gallant Fellow that has dy'd in the Good and Royal Cause; and a small Taste of Happiness will but turn thee off the Ladder with the sadder Heart.

Free.
Hast thou the Conscience, lovely as thou art,
To deal out all thy Beauty to a Traytor?
Is not this Treason of the highest Nature,
To rob the Royal Party of such Treasure
And give it to our mortal Enemies:
For Shame, be wise and just,
And do not live a Rebel to our Cause;
'Tis Sin enough, to have Society with such a wicked Race.

The Roundheads; or, The Good Old Cause

La. Des.
But I am marryed to him.

Free.
So much the worse, to make a League and Covenant with such Villains, and keep the sinful Contract; a little harmless Lying and Dissimulation I'll allow thee, but to be right down honest, 'tis the Devil.

L. Des.
This will not do; it never shall be said I've been so much debauch'd by Conventickling to turn a Sainted Sinner: No, I'm true to my Allegiance still, true to my King and Honour. Suspect my Loyalty when I lose my Virtue; a little Time, I'm sure, will give me honestly into thy Arms, if thou hast Bravery show it in thy Love.

Free.
You will o'recome, and shame me every way;—but when will this Change come? And till it do, what Pawn will you give me? I shall be happy then.

La. Des.
My Honour, and that Happiness you long for; and take but two Months Time for their Redemption.

Free.
How greedily I'll seize the Forfeiture!

La. Des.
But what am I like to get if this Change do come?

Free.
A Slave, and whatever you please to make of him.

La. Des.
Who knows, in such a universal Change, how you may alter too?

Free.
I'll give ye Bond and Vows, unkind *Maria*;—Here, take my hand—Be it known unto all Men, by these Presents, that I *John Freeman* of

London, Gent. acknowledge my self in debt to *Maria Desbro*, the Sum of one Heart, with an incurable Wound; one Soul, destin'd hers from it's first Being; and one Body, whole, sound, and in perfect Health; which I here promise to pay to the said *Maria* , upon Demand, if the aforesaid *John Freeman* be not hang'd before such Demand made. Whereto, I set my Hand,—and seal it with my Lips.

[*in a tone.*

La. Des.
And I, in Consideration of such Debt, do freely give unto the abovesaid *John Freeman* the Heart and Body of the abovesaid *Maria Desbro*, with all Appurtenances thereto belonging, whenever it shall please Heav'n to bring my Husband fairly to the Gallows.

[*in a tone.*

Free.
Amen.—kiss the Book—

[*Kisses her.*

[*Ana. hums without.*

La. Des.
Hah! that's *Ananias* sure; some Danger's near, the necessary Rascal gives us Notice of.

Free.
'tis so, what wou'dst thou have me do?

La. Des.
thou art undone if seen.—Here, step within this Curtain.

[*He goes.*

Enter Ananias, humming, and spreading his Cloak wide; Desbro behind him, puffing in a Chafe.

The Roundheads; or, The Good Old Cause

Des.
Ads nigs, what a Change is here like to be,—puff puff— we have manag'd matters sweetly—to let the *Scotch* General undermine us; puff, puff.

La. Des.
What's the matter?

Des.
Nothing Cockey, nothing, but that we are like to return to our first nothing.

Ana.
Yea verily, when our times come; but ah, the great work of Reformation is not yet fully accomplished, which must be wrought by the saints, and we cannot spare one of them until the Work be finish'd.

Des.
Yea, yea, it is finished I doubt, puff, puff; fye, fye, what a Change is here!

Ana.
Patience, ah, 'tis a precious Virtue!—

Des.
Patience Sir! what, when I shall lose so many fine Estates which did appertain to the Wicked; and which, I trusted, had been establish'd ours; and tell'st thou me of Patience! puff, puff.

[*walking fast.*

Ana.
How lose 'em Sir? Handle the matter with Patience; I hope the Committee of Safety, or the Rump, will not do an illegal thing to one of the Brethren.

Des.
No, No, I have been a trusty Knave to them, and so I have found them all to me: but *Monk! Monk!* O that ever we shou'd be such blind Fools to trust an honest General!

Ana.
Patience Sir, What of him!

Des.
I just now receiv'd private Intelligence, he's coming out of *Scotland* with his Forces.—puff, puff.

Ana.
Why, let him come a Gads Name, we have those will give him a civil Salute, if he mean not honourably to the Commonwealth. Patience Sir.

Des.
But if he prove the stronger, and shou'd chance to be so great a Traytor to us to bring in the Man—the King?

La. Des.
How, the King Husband; the great Heroick?

Free.
Death, this Woman is a Sybill? Ah, Noble *Monk*!

Ana.
Hum—the King!—

Des.
Ah, and with the King, the Bishops; and then, where's all our Church and Bishops Lands! Oh! undone.—puff puff.

Ana.
How, bring in the King and Bishops! my righteous Spirit is raised too:—I say, I will excommunicate him for one of the Wicked; yea, for a prophane Heroick, a Malignant, a Tory,—a—I say, we will surround him, and confound him with a mighty Host; yea, and fight the Lards Battel with him; yea, we will.—

Des.
Truckle to his Pow'r.—puff, puff.

The Roundheads; or, The Good Old Cause

Ana.
Nay, I say verily, nay; for, in Sadness, I will dye in my Calling.

Des.
So I doubt shall I—which is Plowing, Hedging, and Ditching.

Ana.
Yea, we have the Sword of the Righteous in our hand, and we will defend the mighty Revenues of the Church, which the Lard hath given unto his People, and chosen ones—I say, we will defend—

Des.
Ah, Patience, Sir, ah, 'tis a pious Virtue—

Ana.
Ah, it is Zeal in one of us, the out-goings of the Spirit.

Enter Page.

Tom.
Sir, Will you go down to Prayers? the Chaplain waits.

Des.
No, no, Boy, I am too serious for that Exercise,
I cannot now dissemble, Heav'n forgive me.

Ana.
How, Sir, not dissemble—ah, then you have lost a great Vertue indeed, a very great Vertue; ah, let us not give away the Good Old Cause— but, as we have hitherto maintain'd it by Gadly cozenage, and pious frauds, let us persevere—ah, let us persevere to the end; let us not lose our Heritage for a Mess of Pottage, that is, let us not lose the Cause for Dissimulation and Hypocrisie, those two main Engines that have carry'd on the great Work.

Des.
Verily, you have prevailed, and I will go take counsel of my pillow: Boy—call my man to undress me—I'll to bed, for I am sick at heart.

Ex. Tom. Page.

The Roundheads; or, The Good Old Cause

Free.
Death, what shall I do now?

[Des. walks, she whispers Ana.

La. Des.
You must get my man off, or we're undone.

Ana.
Madam, be comforted, Heaven will bring all things about for our advantage.—

[as Des. turns.

La. Des.
But he's behind the Curtains man—

[Des. turns from 'em. spreads his cloak wide and goes by degrees towards the Bed.

Ana.
Ah, let Providence alone— —Your pious Lady, Sir, is doubtful, but I will give her ample satisfaction.

Des.
Ah do, Mr. *Ananias*, do, for she's a good and a vertuous Lady, *certo* she is.

goes close to the Bed-post, and speaks over his shoulder.

Ana.
Get ye behind my cloak—

La. Des.
Indeed Sir, your Counsel and Assistance is very comfortable,

Ana.
We shou'd be helps meet to one another, Madam.

The Roundheads; or, The Good Old Cause

Des.
Alack, good man!

> *[La. Des. goes to cokes her Husb.*

La. Des.
Ay, my Dear, I am so much oblig'd to him, that I know not without thy thy aid, how to make him amends.

Free.
So this is the first Cloak of Zeal I ever made use of.

> *An. going, spreading his cloak to the door, Freeman behind goes out.*

Des.
Good Lady give him this twenty pieces, a dad he worthily deserves 'em.

> *[gives her Gold.*

La. Des.
Indeed, and so he does, Dear, if thou knew'st all. —What say you now, do I not improve in Hypocrisie? and shall I not in time make a precious member of your Church?

> *[to Ana.*

Ana.
Verily, your Ladiship is most ingenious and expert, —Sir, I most humbly take my leave.

> *Ex. Ananias.*

> *Enter Tom Page.*

Page.
My Lord, my Lord *Lambert* has sent in all haste for you, you must attend at his house immediately.

Des.
So, he has heard the News—I must away—let my Coach be ready—

Ex. Des.

La. Des.
How unlucky was this that *Freeman* shou'd be gone—Sirrah, run, and see to o'retake him, and bring him back.

[Ex. all.

Scene II.

A fine Chamber.

Enter Gilliflower and Loveless, by dark, richly drest.

Lov.
Where am I, *Gilliflower*?

Gill.
In my Ladies Apartment, Sir, she'll be with you presently; you need not fear betraying, Sir, for I'll assure you I'm an Heroick in my heart: my Husband was a Captain for his Majesty of ever blessed memory, and kill'd at *Naseby*, God be thanked, Sir.

Lov.
What pity 'tis that thou shou'dst serve this Party?

Gill.
'Bating her Principles, my Lady has good Nature enough to oblige a Servant; and truly Sir, my Vails were good in old *Oliver*'s dayes; I got well by that Amour, between him and my Lady; the man was lavish enough.

Lov.
Yes, of the Nations Treasure—but, prithee tell me, Is not thy Lady mad, raving on Crowns and Kingdoms?

The Roundheads; or, The Good Old Cause

Gill.
It appears so to you, who are not us'd to the Vanity of the Party, but they are all so mad in their degree, and in the Fit they talk of nothing else Sir; we have to morrow a hearing, as they call it.

Lov.
What's that, a Conventicle?

Gill.
No, no, Sir, Ladies of the last Edition, that present their Grievances to the Council of Ladies, of which my Lady's Chief, which Grievances are laid open to the Committee of Safety, and so redress'd, or slighted, as they are.

Lov.
That must be worth one's Curiosity, cou'd one but see't.

Gill.
We admit no man, Sir.

Lov.
'Sdeath, for so good a sight I will turn Woman.
I'll Act it to a hair.

Gill.
That wou'd be excellent.

Lov.
Nay, I must do't: the Novelty is rare—but I'm impatient—prethee let thy Lady know I wait.

Gill.
She's in Affairs of State, but will be here immediately; mean time, retire into her Cabinet, I'll send the Page with Lights, there you may repose, till my Lady comes, on the Pallat.

[*She leads him out.*

The Roundheads; or, The Good Old Cause

Scene III

SCENE. A great Chamber of State, — and Canopy.

And at a Table, seated Lambert, Fleetwood, Desbro, Hewson, Duckingfield, Wariston, Cobbet; all half drunk, with Bottles and Glasses on the Table; La. Lam. and La. Fleet.

Lam.
My Lord *Wariston*, you are not merry to night.

War.
Wons Mon, this *Monk* sticks in my Gullet, the muckle Diel pull him out by th' Lugs; the faud Loone will en spoyle ad our sport mon.

Lam.
I thought I had enough satisfy'd all your Fears; the Army's mine, that is — 'tis yours, my Lords, and I'll employ it too so well for the Good of the Commonwealth, you shall have cause to commend both my Courage and Conduct: my Lord *Wariston*, will you accompany me?

War.
Ah, my gued Lord, the Honour is too great! 'Tis not but I's dare fight my Lord, but I love not the limmer Loone, he has a villainous honest Face an's ene; I's kend him ence, and lik't him not; but I's drink tol yar gued Fortune; let it gang aboote, ene and ad Sirs.

  [all drink.

Lam.
We'll leave all discourse of bus'ness, and give our selves to Mirth; I fancy good Success from this days *Omen*.

  Enter Gill. whispers La. Lam. she rises.

La. Lam.
Waited so long!

The Roundheads; or, The Good Old Cause

Gill.
And grew inpatient, and please your Highness; must I go tell him you cannot see him to Night.

La. Lam.
Not for the World; my silly Politician will be
Busying himself in dull Affairs of State;
—Dull in Comparison of Love, I mean;
I never lov'd before; *Old Oliver* I suffer'd for my Interest,
And!
And 'tis some Greatness, to be Mistress to the best;
But this mighty Pleasure comes *A propo*
To sweeten all the heavy Toyls of Empire.

Gill.
So it does, an't please your Highness.

La. Lam.
Go, let him know I'm coming—Madam, I must beg your Pardon, you hear, my Lord to morrow goes on this great Expedition; and, for any thing we know, may fall a glorious Sacrifice to the Commonwealth; therefore, 'tis meet I offer up some Prayers for his Safety, and all my Leasure Hours 'twixt this and that, will be too few.—Your humble Servant Madam.—

Ex. La. Lam.

La. Fleet.
My Dear, I'll leave you too, my Time of Devotion is come, and heav'n will stay for no Body; where are my People, is my Coach ready, or my Chair.

Fleet.
Go in your Chair my Love, lest you catch cold.

La. Fleet.
And light your Flambeaus,—I love to have my Chair surrounded with Flambeaus.

The Roundheads; or, The Good Old Cause

Enter Page.

Pag.
Your Chair is ready, *Madam*.

[She goes out, led by Fleet.

Hews.
What think ye now my Lords of settling the Nation a little; I find my Head swim with Politicks, and what ye call ums.

War.
Wons, and wad ya settle the Nation when we real our selves?

Hews.
Who, pox shall we stand making Childrens Shoes all the year? No, No, let's begin to settle the Nation, I say, and go throw stich with our Work.

Duc.
Right, we have no Head to obey; so that if this *Scotch* General do come, whilst we Dogs fight for the Bone, he runs away with it.

Hews.
Shaw, we shall patch up matters with the *Scotch* General, I'll warrant you: However, here's to our next Head.—One and All.—

[all drink.

Flee.
Verily Sirs, this Health drinking savoureth of Monarchy, and is a Type of Malignancy.

War.
Bread, my Lord, no preaching o're yar Liquer, wee's now for a Cup o'th' Creature.

Cob.
In a gadly way you may, it is lawful.

The Roundheads; or, The Good Old Cause

Lam.
Come, Come, we're dull, give us some Musick—Come my Lord, I'll give you a Song, I love Musick as I do a Drum, there's Life and Soul in't, call my Musick.

Fleet.
Yea, I am for any Musick, except an Organ.

War.
'SBread Sirs, and I's for a Horn-pipe; I've a faud Theefe here shall dance ye dance tol a Horn-pipe, with any States man a ya'ad.

All.
He, He, He.

Duc.
I know not what your faud Theefe can do; but, I'll hold you a Wager, Collonel *Hewson*, and Collonel *Desbro*, shall dance ye the Saints Jigg with any Sinner of your Kirk, or Field Conventickler.

War.
Wons, and I's catch 'em at that sport, I's dance tol 'em for a *Scotch* Poond but farst yar Song, my Lord, I hope 'tis body, or 'tis not werth a Feart.

All.
He, He, He.

Song sung by Lord Lambert.

A Pox of the States-man that's witty
That watches and Plots all the sleepless Night,
For Seditious Harangues to the Whigs of the City,
And piously turns a Traytor in spight.
Let him wrack and torment his lean Carrion,
To bring his Sham-Plots about,
Till Religion, King, Bishop, and Baron,
For the Publick Good, be quite rooted out.

Whilst we that are no Politicians,
But Rogues that are Resolute, bare-fac'd and Great,

The Roundheads; or, The Good Old Cause

Boldly head the rude Rabble in open Sedition,
Bearing all down before us in Church and in State.
Your Impudence is the best State trick,
And he that by Law means to rule,
Let his History with ours be related,
Tho' we prove the Knaves, 'tis he is the Fool.

War.
The Diel a me, wele sung my Lord, and gen aud Trads fail, yas make a quaint Minstrel.

All.
He, He, He.

War.
Noo Sirs, yar Dance?
>*They fling Cushions at one another, and grin. Musick plays.*

—Mary Sirs, an this be yar dancing, tol dance and ne're stir Stap, the Diel lead the Donce for *Archibald*.
>*When they have flung Cushions thus a while to the Musick Time, they beat each other from the Table, one by one, and fall into a godly Dance; after a while, Wariston rises, and dances ridiculously a while amongst them, then to the Time of the Tune, they take out the rest, as at the Cushion Dance, or in that Nature. Wariston being the last taken in, leads the rest.*

—Haud Minstrels hade; Bread a gued, I's fatch ad Ladies in—lead away Minstrels tol my Ladies Apartment.

[Musick playing before all. Ex. Dancing.

Scene IV

SCENE. *Flat.*

Enter Page.

Pag. Cock.
Here must I wait, to give my Lady Notice when my Lord approaches;—The fine Gentleman that is alone with her, gave me

these two fine pieces of Gold, and bad me buy a Sword to fight for the King withall; and I'm resolv'd to lay it all out in Sword, not a penny in Nickers, and fight for the Heroicks as long as I have a Limb, if they be all such fine Men as this within. But hark, sure I hear some coming.—

    Ex.

    Flat Scene draws off, discovers La. Lam. on a Couch, with Loveless, tying a rich Diamond Bracelet about his Arm; a Table behind with Lights, on which, a Velvet Cushion, with a Crown and Scepter cover'd.

Lov.
This Present's too magnificent: Such Bracelets young Monarchs shou'd put on.

La. Lam.
Persons like me, when they make Presents, Sir, must do it for their Glory, not considering the merit of the Wearer; yet this, my charming *Loveless*, comes short of what I ought to pay thy worth; comes short too of my Love.

Lov.
You bless me, Madam—

La. Lam.
This the great Monarch of the World once ty'd about my Arm, and bade me wear it, till some greater man shou'd chance to win my Heart:

    Thou art that man whom Love hath rais'd above him;
    Whom every Grace and every Charm thou hast
    Conspire to make thee mightier to my Soul;
    And *Oliver*, Illustrious *Oliver*!
    Was yet far short of thee.

The Roundheads; or, The Good Old Cause

Lov.
He was the Monarch then whose Spoils I triumph in.

La. Lam.
They were design'd for Trophies to the young and Gay.
Ah, *Loveless*! that I cou'd reward thy Youth
With something that might make thee more than man,
As well as give the best of Women to thee—
    [rises, takes him by the hand, leads him to the Table. He starts.
—Behold this Gay, this wondrous Glorious thing.

Lov.
Hah—a Crown—and Scepter!
Have I been all this while
So near the Sacred Reliques of my King!
And found no Awful motion in my blood,
Nothing that mov'd Sacred Devotion in me?
    [kneels.

—Hail Sacred Emblem of Great Majesty,
Thou that hast circled more Divinity
Than the great Zodiack that surrounds the World.
I ne'r was blest with sight of thee till now,
But in much reverenc'd Pictures—
    [rises and bows.

La. Lam.
Is't not a lovely thing?

Lov.
There's such Divinity i'th very Form on't,
Had I been conscious I'd been near the Temple
Where this bright Relique of the Glorious Martyr
Had been inshrin'd, 'thad spoil'd my soft Devotion!
—'tis Sacrilege to dally where it is;
A rude, a Sawcy Treason to approach it

The Roundheads; or, The Good Old Cause

With an unbended knee; for Heav's sake, Madam,
Let us not be profane in our Delights,
Either withdraw, or hide that Glorious Object.

La. Lam.
Thou art a Fool, the very sight of this—
Raises my Pleasure higher,
Methinks I give a Queen into thy Arms:
And where I love I cannot give enough;
    [*softly.*

—Wou'd I cou'd set it on thy Head for ever,
'Twou'd not become my simple Lord
The thousandth part so well.
    [*goes to put it on his Head, he puts it back*

Lov.
Forbear, and do not play with holy things,
Let us retire, and love as Mortals shou'd,
Not imitate the Gods, and spoil our Joyes.

La. Lam.
Lovely, and unambitious!
What hopes have I of all your promis'd Constancy,
Whilst this, which possibly 'ere long may adorn my Brow,
And ought to raise me higher in your Love,
Ought to transform you even to Adoration,
Shall poorly make you vanish from it's Lustre;
Methinks the very Fancy of a Queen
Is worth a thousand Mistress's of less Illustrious Rank.

Lov.
What every Pageant Queen? You might from thence infer
I'd fall in Love with every little Actress, because
She acts the Queen for half an hour,
But then the gawdy Robe is laid aside.

The Roundheads; or, The Good Old Cause

La. Lam.
I'll pardon the Comparison in you.

Lov.
I do not doubt your Power of being a Queen,
But trust, it will not last.
How truly brave wou'd your great Husband be,
If whilst he may, he pay'd this mighty Debt
To the Right Owner!
If whilst he has the Army in his Power
He made a true and lawful use of it,
To settle our great Master in his Throne;
And by an act so glorious raise his Name
Even above the Title of a King.

La. Lam.
You love me not, that wou'd perswade me from my Glory.
        Enter *Gilliflower*.

Gill.
Oh, Madam, the Lords are all got merry, as they call it, and are all dancing hither.

La. Lam.
What at their *Oliverian* Frolicks?—dear *Loveless*, withdraw, I wou'd not give the fond believing Fool a Jealousie of me.

Gill.
Withdraw, Madam, 'tis impossible, he must run just into their mouthes.

La. Lam.
Im' ill at these Intrigues, being us'd to Lovers that still came with such Authority, that modestly my Husband wou'd withdraw—but *Loveless* is in danger, therefore take care he be not seen.

Gill.
Heav'ns! they are coming, there's no retreat—

The Roundheads; or, The Good Old Cause

La. Lam.
Lye down on the Couch—and cover him you with the Foot-Carpet,—so, give me my Prayer-Book.
> *He lyes down along on the Couch—they cover him with the Carpet: La. Lam. takes her Book, sits down on his Feet, and leans on the back of the Couch reading; Gill. stands at t'other end; they enter dancing—as before.*

—What Insolence is this? do you not hear me, you—Sots—whom Gayety and Dancing do so ill become.

War. singing.]
Welcom, *Jone Sanderson*, welcom, welcom:
> *[goes to take her out, she strikes him.*
Wons, Madam, that's no part o'th dance.

La. Lam.
No, but 'tis part of a reward for your Insolence, which possibly your Head shall answer for.—

Lam.
Pardon him, my dear, he meant no disrespect to thee.

La. Lam.
How dare you interrupt my Devotion, Sirrah?
Begon with all your filthy ill-bred Crew.
> *[Lam. sits down on Loveless.*

Lam.
My only dear, be patient; hah!
Something moves under me! Treason, Treason.
> *[He rises.*

> *Lov. rouls off, and turns Lam. over, the rest of the men run out crying Treason, Treason, overthrowing the Lights, putting 'em out.*

La. Lam.
Treason, Treason! my Lord, my Lord!

The Roundheads; or, The Good Old Cause

Lam.
Lights there, a Plot, a Popish Plot, lights.
> *She groping about finds Lov. by his clothes knows him.*

La. Lam.
The Crown, the Crown, guard the Crown!
—Here, take this Key, the next room is my Bed-chamber,
Secure your self a moment.—
> *Ex Loveless.*

Lights there, the Crown—who art thou?
> *[takes hold of Lamb.*

Lam.
'Tis I.

La. Lam.
Ah, my Lord, what's the matter?—

Lam.
Nay, my Lady, I ask you what's the matter,

> *Enter Page with lights.*

By Heaven, all is not well: Hark ye, my fine she Politician, who was it you had hid beneath this Carpet?

La. Lam.
Heav'ns! Do'st hear him, *Gilliflower*? Sure the Fellow's mad.

Gill.
Alack, my Lord, Are you out of your Honourable Wits?
Heav'n knows, my Lady was at her Devotion.

Lam.
Bawd, come, confess thy self to be one; at her Devotion, yes, with a He Saint.

The Roundheads; or, The Good Old Cause

Gill.
Ah! Gad forbid the Saints shou'd be so wicked.

La. Lam.
Hark ye, thou little snivelling Hypocrite, who hast no Virtue but a little Conduct in Martial Discipline; who hast by Perjuries, Cheats, and Pious Villanies, wound thy self up into the Rabbles Favour, where thou may'st stand, till some more great in Roguery remove thee from that height, or to the Gallows, if the King return. Hast thou the impudence to charge my Virtue?

Lam.
I know not, Madam, whether that Virtue you boast were lost, or only stak't, and ready for the Gamester; but I am sure a Man was hid under this Carpet.

La. Lam.
Oh Heav'ns, a Man!

Gill.
A Lord, a Man? Are you sure 'twas a man, my Lord?
—Some Villanous Malignant, I'll warrant.

Lam.
It may be so.

Gill.
Alack, the Wickedness of these Heroicks, to hide under Carpets; why they'll have the Impudence to hide under our Petticoats shortly, if your Highness take 'em not down.

> *[To La. Lam.*

Lam.
I do believe so; Death—a Cuckold; shall that black Cloud shade all my rising Fame?

The Roundheads; or, The Good Old Cause

La. Lam.
Cuckold? Why is that Name so great a Stranger to ye,
Or has your rising Fame made ye forget
How long—that Cloud has hung upon your Brow?
—'Twas once the height of your Ambition Sir,
When you—were a poor—sneeking Slave to *Cromwel*:
Then you cou'd cringe and sneere—and hold the Door;
And give him every Opportunity
Had not my Piety defeated your Endeavours.

Lam.
That was for Glory,
Who wou'd not be a Cuckold to be great?
—If *Cromwel* leap'd into my Saddle once,
I'll step into his Throne for't: but, to be pointed at
By Rascals that I—rule,—'tis insupportable.

La. Lam.
How got this Fellow drunk; call up my Officers:
Who dur'st deliver him this Quantity of Wine?
Send straight in my Name, to summon all the
Drunken Committee of Safety to my Presence.
By Heav'n I'll show you Sir—yes they shall
See what a fine King they'r like to have
In Honest, Gadly, Sober, Wise *Jack Lambert*.
—Nay, I'll do't; d'ye think to take away my Honour thus?
I, who by my sole Politicks and Management,
Have set you up Villain of Villains, Sirrah.
—Away—summon 'em all.
    [to Gilliflower.

Lam.
Stay—be not so rash; who was beneath the Carpet?

La. Lam.
I will not answer thee.

The Roundheads; or, The Good Old Cause

Lam.
Nor any living thing?

La. Lam.
No Creature in the Room, thou silly Idiot, but *Gilliflower* and I,—at our Devotion, praying to Heav'n for your Success to morrow;— and am I thus rewarded!

> [*Weeps, Gill. weeps too.*

Lam.
My Soul, I cannot bear the sight of Tears
From these dear charming Eyes.

La. Lam.
No matter Sir, the Committee shall right me.

Lam.
Upon my Knees I ask thy Pardon Dear; by all that's good, I wou'd have sworn I'd felt something stir beneath me, as I sat, which threw me over.

La. Lam.
Only your Brains turn'd round with too much drinking and dancing, Exercises you are not us'd to:—Go sleep, and settle 'em; for I'll not daign to Bed with you to Night;—retire, as 'ere you hope to have my Aid in your Advancement to the Crown.

Lam.
I'm gone,—and once more, pardon my Mistake.

> [*bows, and goes out.*

> [*Ex. Gill.*

La. Lam.
—So, this fighting Fool, so worshipp'd by the Rabble, how meanly can a Woman make him sneeke;

The Roundheads; or, The Good Old Cause

[to Loveless.
—the happy Night's our own.—

Enter Gill. Loveless.

Lov.
Excellent Creature, how I do adore thee!

La. Lam.
But you, perhaps, are satisfy'd already.—

Lov.
Never! shou'dst thou be kind to all Eternity. Thou hast one Vertue more, I pay thee Homage for; I heard from the *Alcove* how great a Mistress thou art in the dear Mystery of Jilting.

La. Lam.
That's the first Lesson Women learn in Conventicles; Religion teaches those Maxims to our Sex, by this!

Kings are depos'd, and Commonwealths are rul'd;
By Jilting all the Universe is fool'd.

ACT V.

Scene I.

Street.

Enter *Corporal, half drest; with Souldiers, Joyner and Felt-maker.*

Cor.
Ha Rogues, the City-Boys are up in Arms; brave Boys, all for the King now!

Felt.
Have a Care what you say Sir; but as to the City's being in Mutiny, that makes well for us: we shall fall to our old Trade of plundering, something will fall to the Righteous, and there is Plunder enough.

Corp.
You plunder Sirrah, knock him down, and carry him into the Guardroom, and secure him.

    [*Two Souldiers seize him.*

1 Sould.
They say, the Committee of Safety sat all Night at General *Lambert's*, about some great Affair—some rare Change Rogues!

2 Sould.
Yes, and to put off Sorrow, they say, were all right reverendly drunk too.

Cor.
I suppose so, there is some heavenly matter in hand; there was Treason cry'd out at the General's last Night, and the Committee of no Safefy all ran away.

The Roundheads; or, The Good Old Cause

1 Sould.
Or rather reel'd away.

Cor.
—The Ladies squeek'd, the Lords fled, and all the House was up in Arms.

Felt.
Yea, and with Reason they say; for, the Pope in disguise was found under the Ladies Bed, and two huge Jesuits as big as the Tall *Irishman*, with Blunderbusses; having, as 'tis said, a design to steal the Crown now in Custody of the General.—

2 Sould.
Good lack, is't possible?

Joyn.
Nay Sir, 'tis true, and is't not time we look'd about us?

Cor.
A Pox upon ye all, for lying Knaves:—secure 'em both on the Guard, till farther Order,—and let us in to th' City-boys: hay for *Lumbard-street*.

2 Sould.
Ay hay for *Lumbard-street*; there's a Shop I have mark'd out for my own already.

1 Sould.
There's a handsom Citizens Wife, that I have an Eye upon, her Husband's a rich Banker, I'll take t'one with t'other.

Joy.
You are mistaken Sir, that plunder is reserv'd for us, if they begin to mutiny; That wicked City that is so weary of a Commonwealth.

2 Sould.
Yes, they'r afraid of the Monster they themselves have made.

The Roundheads; or, The Good Old Cause

Enter Lov. and Free. in disguise.

Cor.
Hah, my Noble Collonel; what, in Disguise!

Free.
We have made our Escapes,—and hope to see better times shortly; the Noble *Scotch* General is come Boys.

Enter Captain of the Prentices, and a great Gang with him, arm'd with Staffs, Swords, &c.

Cap.
Come my Lads, since you have made me Captain, I'll lead you bravely on! I'll dye in the Cause, or bring you off with Victory.

1 Pren.
Here's a Club shall do some Execution; I'll beat out *Hewson*'s t'other Eye; I scorn to take him on the blind Side.

Capt.
In the first Place, we must all sign a Petition to my Lord Mayor.—

2 Pren.
Petitions, we'll have no Petitions Captain; we are for Club Law, Captain.

Cap.
Obey, or I leave you.

All.
Obey, Obey.

Capt.
Look ye, we'll petition for an honest Free Parliament I say.

1 Pren.
No Parliament, no Parliament, we have had too much of that Mischief already Captain.

All.
No Parliament, no Parliament.

Capt.
Farewel Gentlemen, I thought I might have been heard.

Free.
Death Sirs, you shall hear the Captain out.

All.
We obey, we obey.

Capt.
I say, an honest Free Parliament, not one pick'd and chosen by Faction; but such an one shall do our Bus'ness Lads, and bring in the *Great Heroick*.

All.
Ay, Ay, the Great Heroick, the Great Heroick!

Lov.
A fine Youth, and shou'd be encourag'd.

Capt.
Good—in the next place, the noble *Scotch* General is come, and we'll side with him.

Free.
Ay, Ay, all side with him.

1 Pren.
Your Reason, Captain, for we have acted too much without Reason already.

2 Pren.
Are we sure of him, Captain?

Capt.
Oh, he'll doubtless declare for the King, Boyes.

All.
Hay, *Via la Roy, via la Monk.*

Capt.
Next, I hear there's a Proclamation coming out to dissolve the Committee of no Safety.

All.
Good, good.

Capt.
And I hope you are all brave enough to stand to your Loyal Principles with your Lives and Fortunes.

All.
We'll dye for the Royal Interest.

Capt.
In the next place, there's another Proclamation come out.

2 Pr.
This Captain is a man of rare Intelligence; but for what Captain?

Capt.
Why—to—hang us all, if we do not immediately depart to our respective Vocations, how like you that, my Lads?

2 Pr.
Hum—hang'd! I'll e'n home again.

1 Pr.
And I too, I do not like this hanging.

3 Pr.
A man looks but scurvily with his Neck awry.

4 Pr.
Ay, ay, We'll home.

The Roundheads; or, The Good Old Cause

Capt.
Why now you shew what precious men you are—the King wou'd be finely hope up with such Rascals, that for fear of a little hanging wou'd desert his Cause; a Pox upon ye all, I here discharge ye— — take back your Coward Hands, and give me Hearts,

[flings 'em a Scroll.

I scorn to fight with such mean-spirited Rogues.
I did but try your boasted Courages.

Lov.
A brave Boy.

Lov. and Free.
We'll dye with thee, Captain—

All.
Oh, noble Captain, we recant—

1 Pr.
We recant, dear Captain, wee'l dy, one and all.

All.
One and all, once and all.

Capt.
Why so, there's some trusting to you now.

3 Pr.
But is there such a Proclamation, Captain?

Capt.
There is; but anon, when the Crop-ear'd Sheriff begins to read it, let every man inlarge his Voice, and cry, No Proclamation, no Proclamation.

The Roundheads; or, The Good Old Cause

All.
Agreed, agreed.

Lov.
Brave noble Lads, hold still your Resolution,
And when your leisure hours will give ye leave,
Drink the King's Health, here's Gold for you to do so.

Free.
Take my Mite too, brave Lads.
    [*gives 'em Gold.*

All.
Hay! *Viva* the brave Heroicks.
    Enter *Ananias Gogle.*

Ana.
Hum, What have we here, a Street-Conventicle!—or a Mutiny? Yea verily, it is a Mutiny,—What meaneth this appearance in Hostile manner, in open Street, by Day-light?

Capt.
Hah! one of the sanctify'd Lay Elders, one of the Fiends of the Nation, that go about like roaring Lyons, seeking whom they may devour?

Lov.
Who, Mr. *Ananias* the Padder.

Ana.
Bear Witness Gentlemen all, he calls me an High-way Man; thou shalt be hang'd for Scandal on the Brethren.

Lov.
I'll prove what I say, Sirrah; do not you rob on the High-way i'th' Pulpit? Rob the Sisters, and preach it lawful for them to rob their Husbands; rob men even of their Consciences and Honesty; nay, rather than stand out, rob poor Wenches of Bodkins and Thimbles.

The Roundheads; or, The Good Old Cause

Ana.
I commit ye; here Souldiers, I charge ye in the Name of—of— marry I know not who, in my Name, and the good People of *England* , take 'em to safe Custody.

Capt.
How, lay hold of honest Gentlemen! Noble Cavaliers, knock him down.

All.
Knock him down, knock him down.

Free.
Hold worthy Youths; the Rascal has done me Service.

Ana. pulling off his Hat to 'em all.]
Ye look like Citizens, what evil Spirit is entered in unto you, oh men of *London*! that ye have changed your Note, like Birds of evil *Omen*; that you go astray after new Lights, or rather, no Lights, and commit Whoredom with your Fathers Idols, even in the midst of the Holy City, which the Saints have prepared for the Elect, the Chosen ones.

Capt.
Hark ye, Sirrah, leave preaching, and fall to declaring for us, or thou art mortal.

Ana.
Nay, I say nay, I will dye in my Calling—yea I will fall a Sacrifice to the Good Old Cause; abomination ye with a mighty hand, and will destroy, demolish, and confound your Idols, those heathenish Malignants whom you follow, even with Thunder and Lightening, even as a Field of Corn blasted by a strong Blast.

Lov.
Knock him down.

All.
Down with *Dagon*, down with him.

The Roundheads; or, The Good Old Cause

Enter Hewson with Guards.

Hews.
Ah Rogues, have I caught ye napping?

[They all surround him and his Red-Coats.

All.
Whoop Cobler, Whoop Cobler.

The Boys, Lov. and Free. Corp. and Sould. beat off Hewson and his Party. An. gets a Sword, and fights too.

Scene II

SCENE changes to a Chamber.

Enter La. Lam. and Gill.

Gill.
I've had no time to ask your Highness how you slept to night; but that's a needless Question.

La. Lam.
How mean you? do you suspect my Vertue? do you believe *Loveless* dares attempt any thing against my Honour? No *Gilliflower*, he acted all things so like a Gentleman, that every Moment takes my Heart more absolutely.

Gill.
My Lord departed highly satisfied.

La. Lam.
She is not worthy of Intrigues of Love, that cannot mannage a silly Husband as she pleases—but *Gilliflower*, you forget that this is Council day.

Gill.
No but I do not, Madam, some important Suitors wait already.

The Roundheads; or, The Good Old Cause

Enter La. Des. and La. Fleetwood.

La. Lam.
Your Servant, Madam, *Desbro*, thour't welcom—
Gilliflower, are all things ready in the Council Chamber?
We that are Great must sometimes stoop to Acts,
That have at least some shew of Charity;
We must redress the Grievance of our People.

La. Fleet.
She speaks as she were Queen, but I shall put a Spoke in her rising Wheel of Fortune, or my Lords Politicks fail him

[*Scen. draws off, Table with Papers: Chairs round it.*

La. Lam.

Where are the Ladies of the Council?—how remiss they are in their Attendance on us?

La. Fleet.
Us! Heav'ns, I can scarce indure this Insolence!
—We will take care to mind 'em of their Duty—

La. Lam.

We, poor Creature! how simply Majesty becomes her?
[*They all sitting down, Enter La. Cromwel angrily, and takes her Place; Lamb. uppermost.*

—Madam, as I take it, at our last sitting, our pleasure was that you shou'd sit no more.

Crom.
Your pleasure! Is that the General Voice? This is my Place in spight of thee, and all thy fawning Faction, and I shall keep it, when thou, perhaps, shalt be an humble Suppliant here at my Foot-stool.

La. Lam.
I smile at thee.

Crom.
Do, and cringe; 'tis thy bu'sness to make thee Popular—
But 'tis not that,
Nor thy false Beauty that will serve thy Ends.

La. Lam.
Rail on; declining Majesty may be excus'd,
Call in the Women that attend for redress of Grievances.

  Ex. Pag.

 Enter Page with Women, and Loveless dress'd as a Woman.

Gentlewomen, what's your Bu'sness with us?

Lov.
Gentlewomen? some of us are Ladies.

La. Lam.
Ladies, in good time; by what Authority, and from whom do you derive your Title of Ladies?

La. Feet.
Have a care how you usurp what's not your own?

Lov.
How the Devil rebukes Sin?

  [*aside.*

La. Des.
From whom had you your Honours, Women?

Lov.
From our Husbands.

The Roundheads; or, The Good Old Cause

Gill.
Husbands; who are they, and of what standing?

2 Lad.
Of no long standing, I confess.

Gill.
That's a common Grievance indeed.

La. Des.
And ought to be redress'd.

La. Lam.
And that shall be taken into consideration; write it down, *Gilliflower*, Who made your Husband a Knight, Woman?

Lov.
Oliver the first, an't please ye.

La. Lam.
Of horrid Memory; write that down—who yours?

2 La.
Richard the Fourth, an't like your Honour.

Gill.
Of sottish Memory; Shall I write that down too?

La. Des.
Most remarkably.

Cro.
Heav'ns! Can I hear this Profanation of our Royal Family?

    [aside.

La. Lam.
I wonder with what impudence *Noll* and *Dick* cou'd Knightifie your Husbands? for 'tis a Rule in Heraldry, that none can make a Knight but him that is one; 'Tis *Sancha Pancha*'s Case in *Don Quixot*.

Crom.
How dare you question my Husband's Authority?
>[*rises in Anger.*

Who nobly won his Honour in the Field,
Not like thy sneaking Lord, who gain'd his Title
From his Wife's gay Love-tricks,
Bartering her Honour for his Coronet.

La. Lam.
Thou ly'st, my Husband earn'd it with his Sword, braver and juster than thy bold Usurper, who waded to his Glory, through a Sea of Royal Blood.—

La. Des.
Sure *Loveless* has done good on her, and converted her.

La. Fleet.
Madam, I humbly beg you will be patient, You'll ruine all my Lord's Designes else.—Women, proceed to your Grievances, both publick and private.

Lov.
I petition for a Pension, my Husband, deceas'd, was a constant active man, in all the late Rebellion, against the Man; he plunder'd my Lord *Capel*, he betray'd his dearest Friend *Brown Bushel* , who trusted his Life in his hands, and several others; plundering their Wives and Children even to their *Smocks*.

La. Lam.
Most considerable Service, and ought to be consider'd.

2 La.
And most remarkably, at the Tryal of the late Man, I spit in's Face, and betray'd the Earl of *Holland* to the Parliament.

Crom.
In the King's Face, you mean—it shew'd your zeal for the Good Cause.

2 La.
And 'twas my Husband that headed the Rabble, to pull down *Gog* and *Magog*, the Bishops, broke the Idols in the Windows, and turn'd the Churches into Stables and dens of Thieves; rob'd the Altar of the Cathedral of the twelve pieces of Plate call'd the twelve Apostles, turn'd eleven of 'em into Money, and kept *Judas* for his own use at home.

La. Fleet.
On my word, most wisely perform'd, note it down—

3 La.
And my Husband made Libels on the Man, from the first Troubles to this day, defam'd and profan'd the Woman and her Children, printed all the man's Letters to the Woman with Burlesque Marginal Notes, pull'd down the sumptuous Shrines in Churches, and with the golden and Popish Spoils adorn'd his own Houses and Chimney Pieces.

La. Lam.
We shall consider these great Services.

Lov.
To what a height is Impudence arriv'd?

      [aside.

La. Lam.
Proceed to private Grievances.

Lov.
An't please your Honours, my Husband prayes too much; which both hinders his private Bus'ness at home, and his Publick Services to the Commonwealth—

The Roundheads; or, The Good Old Cause

La. Lam.
A double Grievance—set it down, *Gilliflower*.

Lov.
And then he rails against the Whore of *Babylon*, and all my Neighbours think he calls me Whore.

Crom.
A most unpardonable fault.

La. Lam.
We'll have that rectify'd, it will concern us.

Lov.
Then he never kisses me, but he sayes a long Grace, which is more mortifying than inviting.

La. Des.
That is the fault of all the new Saints, which is the reason their Wives take a pious care, as much as in them lies, to send 'em to Heaven, by making 'em Cuckolds.

La. Fleet.
A very charitable work, and ought to be encourag'd.

[*Loveless gives in a Petition to Gilliflower.*

Gill.
The humble Petition of the Lady *Make-shift*,
      [*reads.*
—Heav'ns! Madam, here is many thousand hands to't of the distressed Sex.

All.
Read it.

The Roundheads; or, The Good Old Cause

Gill. reads.]
Whereas there pass'd an Act *June* 24th against Fornication and Adultery, to the great detriment of most of the young Ladies, Gentlewomen, and Commonalty of *England*, and to the utter decay of many whole Families, especially when married to old men; your Petitioners most humbly beg your Honours will take this great Grievance into Mature Consideration and that the said Act may be repealed. —a blessing on 'em, they shall have my hand too.

La. Lam.
We acknowledge, there are many Grievances in that Act: but there are many Conveniences too, for it ties up the Villanous Tongues of men from boasting our Favours.

Crom.
But as it layes a Scandal on Society—'tis troublesom, Society being the very Life of a Republick—*Peters* the first, and *Martin* the Second.

Lov.
But in a Free State, why shou'd not we be free?

La. Des.
Why not? we stand for the Liberty and Property of our Sex, and will present it to the Committee of Safety.

Lov.
Secondly, we desire the Heroicks, vulgarly call'd the Malignants, may not be look'd on as Monsters, for assuredly they are Men; and that it may not be charg'd to us as a Crime to keep 'em company, for they are honest men.

2 L.
And some of 'em men that will stand to their Principles.

La. Lam.
Is there no other honest men that will do as well?

3 La.
Good men are scarce.

The Roundheads; or, The Good Old Cause

La. Lam.
They're all for Heroicks, sure 'tis the mode to love 'em— I cannot blame 'em.

[aside.

Lov.
And that when we go to Mornings and Evenings Lectures, to *Tannlings* or elsewhere, and either before or after visit a private Friend, it may be actionable for the Wicked to scandalize us, by terming of it, abusing the Creature, when 'tis harmless recreating the Creature.

All.
Reason, Reason.

Lov.
Nor that any Husband shou'd interupt his Wife, when at her private Devotion.

Enter Page.

La. Lam.
I have been too late sensible of that Grievance.

Gill.
And Madam, I wou'd humbly pray a Patent for Scolding, to ease my Spleen.

Pag.
An please Your Highness, here's a Messenger arriv'd Post, with Letters from my Lord, the General.

Ex. Pag.

La. Lam.
Greater Affairs—oblige us to break up the Council.

The Roundheads; or, The Good Old Cause

Rises, the Women retire.

Enter Page with Messenger, or Letters.

—What means this Haste?
[Opens, and reads 'em.

Crom.
Hah, bless my Eye-sight, she looks pale,—now red again, some Turn to his Confusion, Heav'n, I beseech thee.

La. Lam.
My Lord's undone! His Army has deserted him;
Left him denfenceless to the Enemies Pow'r.
Ah Coward Traytors! Where's that brutal Courage
That made ye so successful in your Villanies?
Has Hell that taught ye Valour, now abandon'd ye?
—How in an Instant are my Glories fall'n!

Crom.
Ha, ha, ha,—What, has your Highness any cause of Grief?

Gill.
Call up your Courage Madam, do not let these things scoff you,—you may be yet a Queen: Remember what *Lilly* told you Madam.

La. Lam.
Damn *Lilly*, who with lying Prophesies, has rais'd me to the hopes of Majesty: a Legend of his Divels take him for't.

Crom.
Oh, have a Care of Cursing, Madam!

La. Lam.
Screech-Owl, away, thy Voice is ominous.

The Roundheads; or, The Good Old Cause

Oh I cou'd rave! but that it is not great;
—And silent Sorrow—has most Majesty.

Enter Wariston, huffing.

War.
Wons Madam, undone, undone; our honourable Committee is gone to th' Diel, and the damn'd loosey Rump is aud in aud; the muckle Diel set it i'solt, and his Dam drink most for't.

Crom.
The Committee dissolv'd, whose wise Work was that? it looks like *Fleetwood*'s silly Politicks.

War.
Mary, and yar Ladiship's i'th' Right, 'twas en the Work o'th' faud Loone, the Diel brest his Wem for't.

Enter Hewson, Desbro, Whitlock, Duc. and Cob.

Hews.
So Brethren in Iniquity, we have spun a fine Thread, the Rump's all in all now; rules the Rost, and has sent for the General with Sissers and Rasor.

Whit.
With a Sisserara, you mean.

Hews.
None of your Terms in Law, good Brother.

War.
Right, but gen ya have any Querks in Law, Mr. *Lyer*, that will save our Crags, 'twill be warth a Fee.

Duck.
We have plaid our Cards fair.

War.
Is deny that; Wans Sirs ya plaid 'em faul; a Fule had the shooftling of 'em, and the Muckle Diel himself turn'd up Trump.

Whit.
We are lost Gentlemen, utterly lost; who the Devil wou'd have thought of a Desolation?

Hews.
Is there no Remedy?

Duc.
Death, I'le to the *Scotch* General; turn but in time as many greater Rogues than I have done, and 'twill save my Stake yet.—Farewel Gentlemen.

Des.
No Remedy?

War.
Nene Sirs agen the Kings Evel; Bread Sirs, ya's ene gang tol yat Stall agen: Is en follow *Duckingfield*—Farewel *Mr. Leyer* .

La. Lam.
See the Vicissitudes of Humane Glory.
These Rascals, that but Yesterday petition'd me,
With humble Adoration, now scarce pay
Common Civilities due to my Sex alone.
   Enter *Fleetwood.*

Cro.
How now Fool, what is't that makes ye look so pertly? Some mighty Business you have done, I'll warrant.

Fleet.
Verily Lady Mother, you are the strangest Body; a Man cannot please you.—Have I not finely circumvented *Lambert*? Made the

The Roundheads; or, The Good Old Cause

Rump Head, who have committed him to th' Tower; ne're stir now that I have, and I'm the greatest Man in *England*, as I live I am, as a Man may say.

Crom.
Yes, still a greater come. Ah Fool of Fools, not to fore-see the Danger of that nasty Rump.

La. Fleet.
Good Madam, treat my Lord with more Respect.

Crom.
Away fond Fool, born with so little Sense,
To doat on such a wretched Idiot;
It was thy Fate in *Ireton*'s days, to love him,
Or you were foully scandall'd

Fleet.
You are not so well spoken of neither, ne're stir now, and you go to that. I can be King to morrow if I will.

Crom.
Thou ly'st, thou wo't be hang'd first; mark that I tell thee so. I'll prove *Cassandra* to thee, and prophesie thy Doom; Heav'n pays the Traytor back with equal measure. Remember how you serv'd my poor Son *Richard*.

  Ex. Crom. and Page

Flee.
She's mad—Come, my Dear, let's leave the House of this Villain that meant to have couzen'd me illegally of three Kingdoms,—but that I out-witted him at last.

  Ex. Fleet. La. Fleet. and Pag.

La. Lam.
Imprison'd too, i'th' Tower! What Fate is mine?

The Roundheads; or, The Good Old Cause

[leans on Des.

Pag.
Madam, the fine Heroick's come to wait on you.

La. Lam.
Hah, *Loveless*! let him not see the Ruines of my Greatness which he foretold, and kindly begg'd I wou'd usurp no more.

[weep.

Enter *Loveless.*

Lov.
This News has brought me back, I love this Woman! Vain as she is, in spight of all her Fopperies of State—

[bows to her, and looks sad.

La. Lam.
Alas, I do not merit thy Respect,
I'm fall'n to Scorn, to Pity and Contempt.
[weeping.

Ah *Loveless*, fly the Wretched—
Thy Vertue is too noble to be shin'd on
By any thing but rising Suns alone:
I'm a declining shade.—

Lov.
By Heaven, you were never great till now!
I never thought thee so much worth my Love,
My Knee, and Adoration, till this Minute.
[kneels.

—I come to offer you my Life, and all,
The little Fortune the rude Heard has left me.

The Roundheads; or, The Good Old Cause

La. Lam.
Is there such god-like Vertue in your Sex?
Or rather, in your Party.
Curse on the Lies and Cheats of Conventicles,
That taught me first to think Heroicks Divels,
Blood-thirsty, lewd, tyrannick Salvage Monsters.
—But I believe 'em Angels all, if all like *Loveless*.
What heavenly thing then must the Master be,
Whose Servants are Divine?
    Enter *Page running.*

Pag.
Oh Madam! all the Heroick-Boys are up in Arms, and swear they'll have your Highness, dead or alive,—they have besieg'd the House.

La. Lam.
Heavens, the Rabble!—those faithless things that us'd to crowd my Coaches Wheels, and stop my Passage, with their officious Noise and Adoration.

  Enter *Freeman.*

Free.
Loveless, Thy Aid; the City-Sparks are up;
Their zealous Loyalty admits no Bounds.
A glorious Change is coming, and I'll appear now bare fac'd.

Lov.
Madam, fear not the Rabble; retire, *Freeman* and I can still 'em.
    [leads her in, and bows low.

Free.
My dear *Maria*, I shall claim ye shortly—

L. D.
Do your worst, I'm ready for the Challenge
    [go in.

    Ex. Lov. and Free. another way.

The Roundheads; or, The Good Old Cause

Scene III

SCENE. *The Street.*

Enter Captain and the rest.

Capt.
I say we'll have the She-Polititian out, she did more mischief than her Husband, pittiful, dittiful *Lambert*; who is, thanks be praised, in the Tower, to which place, Lord of his mercy bring all the Kings Enemies.

All.
Amen, Amen.

Enter Lov. and Freeman.

Lov.
Why how now Captain, what besiege the Women? No, let us lead our Force to Nobler Enemies.

Cap.
Nay, noble Chief, your word's our Law.

Lov.
No, I resign that Title to the brave *Scotch* General, who has just now enter'd the City.

Cap.
We know it, Sir; Do you not observe how the Crop-ear'd Phanaticks trot out of Town?—The Rogues began their old belov'd Mutiny, but 'twou'd not do.

Lov.
A Pox upon 'em, they went out like the Snuff of a Candle, stinkingly and blinkingly.

1 Pr.
Ay, ay, let 'em hang themselves, and then they are cold meat for the Devil.

The Roundheads; or, The Good Old Cause

Cap.
But noble Champion, I hope we may have leave to rost the Rump to Night?

Lov.
With all our hearts; here's Money to make Fires—

Free.
And here's for drink too't, Boyes.

All.
Hey—*Via le Roy, via les Heroicks*!

> [*go out hollowing.*
>
> *Enter Ananias peeping, Felt. and Joyner.*

Ana.
So, the Rabble's gone: ah, Brethren! what will this wicked World come too?

Felt.
Alack, alack, to no goodness, you may be sure; pray what's the News?

> [*Fleet peeping out of a Garret Window.*

Fleet.
Anania, Anania.

Ana.
Who calleth *Ananias*? lo, here am I.

Fleet.
Behold, it is I, look up. How goeth tidings?

Ana.
Full ill, I fear, 'tis a bad Omen to see your Lordship so nigh Heaven; when the Saints are Garettifi'd.

Fleet.
I am fortifying my self against the Evil day.

Ana.
Which is come upon us like a Thief in the Night; like a Torrent from the Mountain of Waters; or a Whirl-wind from the Wilderness.

Flee.
Why, what has the *Scotch* General done?

Ana.
Ah! He playeth the Devil with the Saints in the City, because they put the Covenant Oath unto him, he pulls up their Gates, their Posts and Chains, and enters.

Felt.
And wou'd the wicked City let him have his beastly will of her?

Ana.
Nay, but she was ravished—deflow'red.

Joyn.
How, ravish'd! oh, monstrous! was ever such a Rape committed upon an innocent City? lay her Legs open to the wide World, for every Knave to view her Nakedness?

Felt.
Ah, ah! what Dayes, what Times, and what Seasons are here?

Enter Capt. Corporal, and Prentices, with faggots, hollowing.

Corp.
What say you now, Lads, is not my Prophesie truer than *Lillie* 's? I told you the Rump wou'd fall to our handling, and drinking for: the Kingss proclaim'd, Rogues.

Cap.
Ay, ay, *Lilly*, a Plague on him, he prophesied *Lambert* shou'd be uppermost.

Cor.
Yes, he meant perhaps on *Westminster* Pinacle; where's *Lilly* now, with all his Prophecies against the Royal Family?

Capt.
In one of his Twelve Houses.

1 Pr.
We'll fire him out to night, Boy; come, all hands to work for the Fire.

Exeunt all, hollowing.

Fleet.
Ah, dismal, heavy day, a day of Grief and Wo,
Which hast bereft me of my hopes for ay, ah Lard, what shall I do?
Exit.

Scene IV

SCENE. *A Chamber.*

Enter Lov. leading La. Lam. in disguise, Page and Gilliflower disguis'd, Lov. dressing her.

Lov.
My Charmer, why these Tears?
If for the fall of all thy painted Glories,
Thou art, in the esteem of all good men,
Above what thou wer't then:
The glorious Sun is rising in our Hemisphere,
And I, amongst the crowd of Loyal Sufferers,
Shall share in its kindly Rayes.

La. Lam.
Best of thy Sex—
What have I left to gratifie thy goodness?

Lov.
You have already by your noble Bounty

Made me a Fortune, had I nothing else;
All which I render back, with all that Wealth
Heaven and my Parents left me:
Which, tho' unjustly now detain'd from me,
Will once again be mine, and then be yours.

Enter Free.

Free.
Come, haste, the Rabble gather round the House,
And swear they'll have this Sorceress.

Lov.
Let me loose among 'em, their rude officious honesty must be punish'd.

La. Lam.
Oh, let me out, do not expose thy Person to their mad rage, rather resign the Victim.

[holds him.

Lov.
Resign thee! By Heaven, I think I shou'd turn Rebell first.

Enter La. Des. disguis'd, and Page, with Jewels in a Box.

La. Des.
With much ado, according to thy direction, dear *Freeman*, I have pass'd the Pikes, my House being surrounded, and my Husband demanded, fell down dead with fear.

Free.
How, thy Husband dead!

La. Des.
Dead as old *Oliver*! and much ado I got off with these Jewels, the Rabble swore I was one of the Party, and had not the honest

Corporal convinc'd 'em, I had been pull'd to pieces:—Come, haste away, Madam, we shall be rosted with the Rump else.

La. Lam.
Adieu, dear Mansion! whose rich gilded Roofs so oft put me in mind of Majesty—And thou my Bed of State, where my soft Slumbers have presented me with Diadems and Scepters,—when waking I have stretch'd my greedy Arms to grasp the vanish'd Phantom! ah, adieu! And all my hopes of Royalty adieu.—

Free.
And dare you put your self into my Protection? Well, if you do, I doubt you'll never be your own Woman again.

La. Des.
No matter, I'm better lost than found on such occasions.

Exeunt.

Scene V

SCENE, a Street; a great Bonfire, with Spits, and Rump rosting, and the Mobile about the Fire, with Pots, Bottles, and Fiddles.

1 Pren.
Here, *Jack*, a Health to the King.

2 Pren.
Let it pass, Lad, and next to the Noble General.

1 Pren.
Ralph, baste the Rump well, or ne'r hope to see a King agen.

3 Pr.
The Rump will baste it self, it has been well cram'd.

Enter *Freeman, La. Des. Loveless,* and *La. Lam. Gill. Pages,* &c.

The Roundheads; or, The Good Old Cause

Capt.
Hah, Noble Champion, Faith Sir, you must honour us so far as to drink the King's Health, and the Noble General's before you go.

> *Enter Wareston, drest like a Pedlar, with a Box about his Neck full of Ballads and things.*

War.
Will ya buy a Guedly Ballat or a Scotch Spur Sirs? a guedly Ballat or a Scotch Spur.—S'bread, Is scapt hither te weele enough, Is sav'd my Crag fro stretching twa Inches longer than 'twas borne: will ya buy a Jack line to rost the Rump, a new *Jack Lambert* line,—or a blithe Ditty, of the Noble Scotch General—come buy my Ditties.

Capt.
How a Ditty o'th' General? let's see't, Sirrah.

War.
S'bread, Sirs, and here's the guedly Ballad of the General's coming out of *Scotland*.

Capt.
Here, who sings it? we'll all bear the bob.

> *[Wariston sings the Ballad, all bearing the Bob.*
>
> *Enter Ananias, crying Almanacks.*

Ana.
New Almanacks, new Almanacks.

Cap.
Hah, who have we here? *Ananias Holder-forth* of *Clements* Parish?

All.
Ha, a Traytor, a Traytor.

The Roundheads; or, The Good Old Cause

Lov.
If I be not mistaken, this blithe Ballad-singer too was Chair-man to the Committee of Safety.

Capt.
Is your Lordship turn'd Pedlar at last?

War.
What mon I do noo? Lerd, ne mere Lerd than yar sel Sir; wons Is show 'em a fair pair a heeles.

> *goes to run away, they get him on a Coltstaff, with Ananias on another, Fidlers playing Fortune my Foe round the Fire.*

Capt.
Play Fortune my Foe, Sirrah.

> *Enter Hewson, drest like a Country-Fellow.*

Cor.
Who are you, Sirra? you have the mark o'th' Beast.

Hews.
Who, aye, Sir? aye am a Doncer, that come a merry making among ya—

Cap.
Come, Sirrah, your Feats of Activity quickly then.

> *[He dances, which ended, they get him on a colt-staff, and cry a Cobler, a Cobler.*

All.
A Cobler, a Cobler.

Capt.
To Prison with the Traytors, and then we have made a good Nights work on't.

The Roundheads; or, The Good Old Cause

Then let's all home, and to the Powers Divine,
Pray for the King, and all the Sacred Line.